Elizabeth Watts

The Orchard and Fruit Garden

Their culture and produce

Elizabeth Watts

The Orchard and Fruit Garden
Their culture and produce

ISBN/EAN: 9783337069018

Printed in Europe, USA, Canada, Australia, Japan

Cover: Foto ©Lupo / pixelio.de

More available books at **www.hansebooks.com**

Frederick Warne & Co., Publishers.

Dictionaries.

In small crown 8vo, price 2s. 6d., cloth; or half calf, 5s.
THE STANDARD PRONOUNCING DICTIONARY OF THE ENGLISH LANGUAGE.
Based on the Labours of WORCESTER, WEBSTER, OGILVIE, RICHARDSON, CRAIG, GOODRICH, JOHNSON, WALKER, and TRENCH. Comprising *many thousand New Words*, which Modern Literature, Science, Art, and Fashion have called into Existence. Edited by P. AUSTIN NUTTALL, LL.D.

Edited by P. A. NUTTALL, LL.D.
Large demy 18mo, 288 pp., price 1s., cloth gilt; roan, 1s. 6d.
WALKER'S PEARL DICTIONARY.
Edited throughout from the most recent approved Authorities.

In crown 8vo, price 1s., cloth gilt; leather, 1s. 6d.
JOHNSON'S SHILLING DICTIONARY MODERNIZED.
Edited from the most Approved Authorities.

In crown 48mo, price 1s., cl. limp, 640 pp.; roan, gilt edges, 1s. 6d.
WARNE'S BIJOU DICTIONARY.
Pearl Type, with Portrait of DR. JOHNSON. Edited from the Authorities of JOHNSON, WALKER, WEBSTER, RICHARDSON, WORCESTER, SHERIDAN, &c.

In 18mo, cloth boards, price 6d., 290 pp.; or half roan, 1s.
WARNE'S POPULAR EDITION OF
WALKER'S PRONOUNCING DICTIONARY,
with Webster's Definitions and Worcester's Improvements.

READY RECKONERS.—New Type, New Endings.
In demy 18mo, 1s., cloth; leather, 1s. 6d.
THE MODEL READY RECKONER.
With Interest and Commission Tables. 50th Thousand.

And, price 6d. each, cloth lettered.
WARNE'S BIJOU READY RECKONER. Royal 32mo.
WARNE'S LARGE TYPE READY RECKONER. Demy 18mo.

In crown 8vo, 2s. 6d., cloth; roan, 3s. 6d.
THE AVOIRDUPOIS WEIGHT CALCULATOR
AND READY RECKONER; with Interest and Discount Tables. By ARTHUR EDWARD KING, Accountant.

Bedford Street, Covent Garden.

Frederick Warne & Co., Publishers.

Alphabets, Primers, Readers, &c.

In imperial 16mo, price 6d. each, fancy covers.

WARNE'S ALPHABET AND WORD BOOK. With Four Coloured Plates (KRONHEIM'S Process).

WARNE'S SPELLING AND READING BOOK. With Four Coloured Plates (KRONHEIM'S Process).

WARNE'S PRIMER. With Two Coloured Pictures.

In crown 8vo, price 6d. cloth cover.

MAVOR'S ILLUSTRATED PRIMER. With Three Hundred and Fifty Pictures.

In demy 8vo, price 1s. each, cloth, gilt lettering.

THE VICTORIA PICTURE SPELLING BOOK. With Three Hundred and Eighty-four Illustrations.

THE VICTORIA PICTURE READING BOOK. Compiled and Edited by L. V. With numerous Illustrations.

Demy 8vo, price 1s. cloth covers.

EVERLASTING VICTORIA PRIMER. 150 Illustrations, printed on fine Linen.

EASY READING FOR ADULT LEARNERS. In Words of One Syllable. In fcap. 8vo, cloth boards. By CAROLINE HOLROYD. Compiled especially for the Use of Evening Schools.

POPULAR ENGLISH SPELLING BOOKS.

In fcap. 8vo, NINEPENCE each, strongly bound, cloth or tin rims.

MAVOR'S BRITISH SPELLING BOOK.
GUY'S Ditto.
CARPENTER'S Ditto, with Meanings.
FENNING'S UNIVERSAL Ditto.
VYSE'S NEW LONDON Ditto.
MARKHAM'S USEFUL Ditto.

Also, SUPERIOR EDITIONS, post 8vo, ONE SHILLING, cloth, of
MAVOR'S SPELLING BOOK.
GUY'S BRITISH SPELLING BOOK.
CARPENTER'S Ditto, with full Accentuation.

In fcap. 8vo, 9d., strongly bound.

WALKINGHAME'S ARITHMETIC; Modernized, Revised, and Corrected, by E. LETHBRIDGE, M.A., late Scholar and Exhibitioner of Exeter College, Oxford, and Special Tutor to the Civil Service Examinations.

THE KEY TO WALKINGHAME, 3s. 6d.

Bedford Street, Covent Garden.

1. Common Gooseberry Blossom.
2. Ribes tubulosum, or Mignon Gooseberry.
3. Common Currant Blossom.
4. Ornamental Flowering Currant.
5. Plymouth Strawberry.
6. Wood Strawberry.
7. Chili Strawberry.

THE ORCHARD AND FRUIT GARDEN:

Their Culture and Produce.

BY

ELIZABETH WATTS,

AUTHOR OF "FLOWERS AND THE FLOWER GARDEN,"
"VEGETABLES, AND HOW TO GROW THEM."

LONDON:
FREDERICK WARNE & CO.,
BEDFORD STREET, COVENT GARDEN.

PREFACE

We have so many excellent large and expensive works on fruit culture, that I should never have thought of writing this one, if its peculiar place had not stood vacant, waiting to be filled. It is the first *cheap work* on the Orchard and Fruit Garden. Those who, like myself, have had through life some space of land, between a pole and an acre, at command, do not need to be puzzled with lists of hundreds in the selection of the trees they want; their need is one which I have made it my endeavour to supply, *i.e.* particulars of a *few* good sorts of fruit trees of all kinds which any careful cultivator can manage, and which may be obtained at any good nursery. The sorts named are good, those I most recommend I have tested, and the directions given respecting their cultivation will be found plain, concise, and practical. I can only hope my little book will be found useful to all who delight in fruit culture, but who cannot command access to voluminous and expensive works upon the subject.

E. WATTS.

Jersey, May, 1867.

CONTENTS.

Chapter		Page
I.	The Orchard	1
II.	Choosing and Planting	5
III.	Propagation and Improvement	10
IV.	Grafting and Budding	15
V.	Culture of Fruit trees.—Pruning	25
VI.	Training	30
VII.	Protection	37
VIII.	Diseases and Insects	42
IX.	Tools and Storing-rooms	55
X.	The Pear Tree and its Produce	60
XI.	Summer and Autumn Pears	65
XII.	Keeping Pears	72
XIII.	Pears of the Last Century	79
XIV.	Quinces and Baking Pears	82
XV.	Apples	86
XVI.	Keeping Apples	97
XVII.	Almonds	105
XVIII.	Apricots	106
XIX.	Peaches	111
XX.	Varieties of Peaches	116
XXI.	Varieties of Nectarines	122
XXII.	Plums, good kinds	126
XXIII.	Cherries	136
XXIV.	Useful kinds	139
XXV.	Gooseberries and Currants	145
XXVI.	A few good Gooseberries	150
XXVII.	Varieties of Currants	154
XXVIII.	Raspberries	156
XXIX.	Strawberries	160
XXX.	Mulberries, Medlars, and Nuts	165
XXXI.	Figs	171
XXXII.	Vines for out of doors	174
XXXIII.	Melons	181

THE

ORCHARD AND FRUIT GARDEN.

CHAPTER I.

THE ORCHARD.

In the treatment of our fruit trees, sins of omission are more general than sins of commission. Whereas many, in the present advanced state of Horticulture, select with precision, plant with care, prune with skill, manure sufficiently, and accommodate the soil to the development and improvement of the fruit, there are yet also many others who seem to think a tree a tree, and one about as good as another, make a hole in which to bury the root, together with all reasonable hope of success, and leave the rest to nature and to chance. This negligent gardening, although still too prevalent, is much less so than formerly. Excellent treatises and well-conducted periodicals now aid the beginner with advice and instruction, and offer a theatre for the discussion of all moot points. These valuable works are, however, not so universally within the reach of all fruit growers and lovers of a garden as to render a cheap work on the management of fruit trees superfluous.

Fruit fresh gathered and good in kind, is so pleasant and so useful an addition to diet, and so especially valuable in the case of children and young people, that I can scarcely comprehend why there are so many gardens, even of the smallest dimensions, entirely without fruit trees, and why ground, where they would grow, thrive, and produce, is often devoted to trees which are not more ornamental than they, and which entirely lack their utility. I scarcely like to see even an ornamental flowering shrub or tree occupying a fine wall which might be utilized in the production of good stone fruit or pears, with very little loss on the score of decoration; but this is merely a matter of fancy.

"Be aye sticking in a tree," was the Scottish Laird's instruction to his heir, "it will be growing, Jock, when ye're sleeping," and "be aye putting in a fruit tree," I echo, after trying the plan with five different residences, situated in various localities, soils, and climates, occupied and tested during the last quarter of a century.

An outcry against a man for *selfishness*, because he shows an unwillingness to plant trees in ground not his own, is hardly fair, since few wish to practise unsolicited bestowal of property on unknown recipients; but as a matter affecting personal remuneration, it is not necessary or prudent to avoid planting because we may have no permanent or lengthened hold on the land we occupy. If our tenure expire soon or unexpectedly, we have, I believe, the right by law to remove trees within three years of the time of planting them, and when they have been planted more than that time, those which have been chosen, planted, and managed with judgment, will already have made a fair return on outlay and work. A well-managed tree will within a *very* few years of the time of planting prove a capital investment, and one the interest of which will continually increase for many years; I therefore very strongly recommend all who own or rent a bit of ground, to plant trees; if the tenure be given up soon, the trees can be removed, and the removal will do them no harm; and if they are held for from three to a dozen years, they will in that time make a much better return than any other crop which can be grown.

If the tenure be short or uncertain, fruits which will make an early return may be planted,—such as apples, gooseberries, currants, raspberries, strawberries, and perhaps some well-chosen stone fruit trees. If the tenure be pretty secure, and of unlimited duration, then plant without reservation pears, and all other choice fruits, only taking care to plant so far apart as to leave ample space for the increase of every tree that is planted.

The best situation for an orchard or fruit garden is a gentle slope towards the South, South-east, or East. A North aspect should be avoided, and a West aspect is too much open to tearing winds, and too burning in the afternoon heat to be beneficial. A low, damp situation should be avoided, as no tree will do well and produce fine fruit if its roots are occasionally in water. At the same time a low, sheltered spot, if dry, is better than exposed high land, being less open to cold, and violent wind.

With regard to soil, good corn land is said to do well for fruit; good loam is best. The soil should be neither too light and dry, nor too heavy and stubborn; if its nature require such treatment, it should be trenched and drained, and its surface should have a sufficient thickness of fine, fertile earth.

An orchard may be stocked with apples, pears, cherries, or plums. In the fruit garden we may have these and all other fruits; the vinery, orchard house and frame will give choice fruit earlier than it can be produced out of doors, and every good wall should be made available for apricots, peaches, and nectarines, and the choicest kinds of pears, plums, and cherries.

If grass land be used as an orchard, it must not be imagined that all may be taken from the land and nothing restored to it. The earth pays double dues in fruit and grass, and therefore it cannot be expected to do its duty and produce fine crops and fine fruit too, unless it be doubly manured: manured on the score of the fruit trees, and again on that of the green or other crop which is taken off it.

The same may be said of fruit gardens which are also used to grow vegetables. If the vegetables are dug and removed without mercy on the fruit trees, their roots will be injured and impoverished, and their fruit spoiled. The digging must be managed with reference to the roots of the trees, and no crop must be put in so close to a tree as to interfere with it either while it grows or in its removal. The manure, too, must not be given to the vegetables without regard to the prosperity of the trees; it must on no account be given close round the roots at a season when forcing them would encourage rampant growth to the detriment of a fine crop of fruit, nor withheld from them when mulching is requisite or beneficial.

Fruit and vegetables, or fruit and orchard crops, may do well in concert if all are fairly treated, and fairly enriched, but for the production of choice fruit it should be made the *specialité* in either the orchard or the garden.

For fencing, there is nothing that may be compared with fine, smooth, high walls, as available for the training of the best kinds of fruit, and a safeguard against the depredations of thieves. Next to these in merit, though far inferior, stand well-made, close wooden fences, and these are about the only methods of enclosure to be used with advantage for orchards or fruit gardens.

A wall should be at least eight feet high, and as much higher as can be made convenient. If not more than eight feet, it may be nine inches in thickness. From eight to fourteen feet high requires thirteen inches and a half in thickness, and above that height eighteen inches. A wall, if high and many feet in length, must be strengthened with buttresses, and the foundation of all walls should be a brick and a half thick, even where the wall itself is only one brick thick.

Flued or hot walls are built hollow, the interstices being used as flues for the circulation of artificial heat. It is necessary for these walls to have hooks along, near the top, under the coping, or other apparatus for arranging protection over the trees when necessary.

A wall like this will require a fire to every forty or fifty feet of wall. Stone walls are good, but they almost require a lattice over them to which to train trees.

All the walls of a fruit garden may be made valuable, even that with the North aspect being needed for shelter, and available for Morello cherries, and some other fruits.

A well-formed, well-kept bank, with a hedge at the top regularly pruned and thickened, is a good fence to an orchard in the country, especially if the locality be cheap in labour, and dear in bricks and other building commodities.

For hedges to a fruit garden, evergreens only can be tolerated, and they are so inferior in utility to walls of any kind that they should never be used unless as a positive matter of necessity.

A nursery for rearing and testing young trees is a valuable adjunct to every establishment where fruit is much thought of: there we can bring forward young trees for future use, increase the choice sorts, try the merits of all which are unknown, and provide stocks for any valuable varieties that may be met with.

CHAPTER II.

CHOOSING AND PLANTING.

FIVE out of every six persons who become possessed of a garden find it already planted to their hands. What they have to do is to wait and watch in the first instance, lest the indiscriminate rooting up of untried trees effect a work of destruction instead of improvement. Even old and apparently worn-out trees had better be spared for a year, and encouraged into bearing, that the owner, if cutting them up be thought best, may know what he destroys.

Careful cleansing, liberal pruning, judicious manuring, and scientific general treatment, have rendered many trees which were queer old things to look at, productive and valuable; and, on the other hand, numbers are ruthlessly destroyed without need, and gardens thrown back years in productiveness by the process.

Where there is space for the introduction of new trees, the choice must be made with care, and with reference not only to the selection of the trees, but to the applicability of the kind to the locality, and the position intended for them. By a little inspection of gardens near, information may generally be obtained as to fruits that are quite unlikely to thrive, and as to the kinds most likely to do well. Any person may decide without much reflection that it can only lead to disappointment to plant trees of a delicate kind in a sharp, bleak, or cold damp situation, or to put those which are easily injured by smoke in the immediate neighbourhood of London or any other large town.

Apples will do in most garden soils and in most localities, provided the ground be tolerably well drained, and gooseberries and currants may prosper where trees of larger growth fail to produce. Wall fruit, pears, plums, and cherries, require warm sheltered spots, or the nipping frosts of spring will destroy their crops year after year.

Young trees, recently grafted, are generally purchased, but if they are of three or four years' standing, and are transplanted with care, the additional outlay will be repaid by their earlier productiveness. Choose young trees of a free, vigorous growth, avoiding those with a weakly, run appearance, and a thick growth of thin sprays.

For the kind, in purchasing young trees, we must depend in a great degree on the honesty and precision of the man we buy of. It is a good plan to make the selection early enough in the autumn to see the fruit on the trees, and then to mark each one which is chosen with a plain and unmistakable tally, carried for the purpose by the buyer, and affixed firmly and immovably by him. With this care no *mistake* can well interfere with the delivery of the right trees at the right season. A label with the name of the buyer *cut* on it is about the best and most unmistakable mark to use for this purpose.

Even while quite young, the trees should have an equal,

regular, well-balanced growth; for those which are irregular, one-sided, or cluttered in the branches will never, without care, time, and trouble, develop into trees of elegant form. In young wall or espalier trees, take especial care that the sprays are even and regular.

A thoroughly healthy appearance in the trees, in bark and foliage, must also be carefully looked to. Never choose any with moss-grown, foul, unhealthy-looking bark, or with American blight, canker, or any other destructive growth, insect, or disease, but notice that the bark is delicate in texture, smooth (according to kind) and clean.

Canker is an evil which has annually destroyed numbers of our finest fruit trees, especially pears. It comes from old age, but in young trees it often proceeds from bruises or other ill usage. Trees planted in an uncongenial soil, and those that are pruned in a bad, slovenly manner, are very subject to the disease. It begins with a swelling of the bark and wood in some one particular spot. In a certain number of years, few or many, according to the favourable or unfavourable circumstances under which the tree exists, the alburnum (or layers of young wood next to the bark, in which are placed the vessels for the circulation of the sap) perishes, and the bark on the spot cracks, rises in discoloured scales, and decays rapidly, circulation is interrupted, and all the portion of the tree above the canker dies. Take care never to buy trees with an appearance of this disease, nor to induce it by careless bruising and wounding, by allowing branches to cross and chafe each other, by planting in an ungenial soil, nor by humouring an over-rampart growth.

The American blight is a very destructive aphis which attacks apple trees especially, but other trees also at times. It may be detected in a moment by the appearance of a perfectly white cottony matter in the cracks and inequalities of the bark, which form its home. This cottony substance flies on the wind from tree to tree, and so spreads the evil; and the insect, like other aphides, is said to have wings at its season.

When the trees are bought, the next thing is to plant them. Dig and trench the earth, where a tree is to be planted, or a plantation made, three feet deep; if the subsoil be too wet, the ground should be drained, and if it be poor, remove it and replace it with good, moderately rich loam.

October is the best time for planting, but any period between that and the first breath of spring, *i.e.*, while the trees are near or in their winter rest, will do. Any week in November, December, or January, provided the weather be so open as to present no danger of sharp frost, is good, but the *best* time is before the growth of the tree has entirely ceased for the season, because the impulse of growth, to replace the spongelets of the roots which are injured, is beneficial to its restoration, after the trial of transplanting.

Take care that the tree is not planted with the earth loosely thrown in, or, as the mould sinks, and the root with it, the tree will be too deep in the earth. Neither let the mould be stamped in too hard, to bruise the roots and prevent the ingress of air and water.

Make the hole for a young tree of medium size, four feet across each way, renew the subsoil, if necessary or advisable, and have ready good earth, properly enriched, with which to fill up. Before placing the tree, stamp the bottom of the hole flat and firm, to discourage the roots from running down too deep. If, the tree has previously been well planted, or well rooted, disturb it as little as possible, but remove it with as large a ball of earth as can be, undisturbed round the root. If, on the other hand, it has been badly planted, is removed from a bad soil, or needs root-pruning, on account of too rampant growth, or canker on the root, shake off the earth, fill in the hole just so that the lowest of the roots can be spread abroad in their natural position and elevation, placing the collar of the tree above the natural surface of the ground. Fill in the earth over the first layer of roots, spread another layer and fill in, and continue the same until all the roots are spread in their right position and right elevation. Throw in the earth in the direction of the roots, not from the outside towards the bole, so as to turn back some of the tender rootlets from their right direction. As soon as the roots are covered, water plentifully with a rose on the watering-pot, and then finish filling in the earth. If a tree be large and branching, the branches must be compactly tied up before its removal, and a good stake must be firmly placed before the roots are covered, lest in driving it in, some of them get injured. A little cavity may be left round the bole to retain the water afterwards given.

In transplanting, the circumstances especially demanding care are to save injury to the delicate organs of the roots, and to prevent injurious evaporation. A little injudicious violence to the tender rootlets will do great mischief to a tree or plant; and to prevent evaporation, time should be chosen when neither earth nor air are excessively dry.

Where the soil, especially the subsoil, is not favourable for the kind of tree to be planted, what gardeners term planting on stations, *i.e.*, planting on a paved foundation, is found advantageous. Where the land is of a nature to require more efficient draining than the cultivator may wish to bestow on it, trees may prosper with this kind of planting which would otherwise fail. In a moist soil, inefficiently drained, the trees may be planted in a shallow hole, and the earth may be raised round them above the natural level of the ground; but if the locality be dry, they may be planted with the collar well above the ground line. Dig a hole six feet square: two feet deep will be enough for trees which are to be kept to a dwarf habit of growth, but four or five inches more must be removed to make room for the paving material (if I may call it so) to be introduced. In digging the hole, throw all the good rich earth together to use again, and remove entirely all the clayey, sour subsoil, to be replaced with good, appropriate, rich mould in the planting. Beat the bottom of the hole flat, and fill in with four or five inches thickness of refuse stone from a quarry, brickbats, chalk, or clinkers: some persons recommend paving-stones for the purpose. Ram down the surface hard, and spread over it a covering of riddled cinders, or gravel, and this paving will pretty effectually keep the roots of the trees from straying into the bad soil below. To make up for bad soil removed, add to the best of the earth dug out whatever the ground most requires, and let it be of the kind fitted to the trees. A naturally dry, sandy soil will be improved by a mixture of clayey loam, and a clay soil will require sandy loam, or road-sweepings; and the parings of commons and the sides of roads and lanes will improve it.

In planting, take especial care to keep the collar of the tree well above the surface of the ground.

The manure given to enrich the spot should be of the most lasting kind. Nothing is better for the purpose than turf; and as its decaying vegetation is its manuring principle, it may be taken from poor land: dry refuse vegetable matter, such as bean and pea haulm, old thatch or straw, will do, and if animal manure be used, let it be fresh from the stable or cow-house; but introduce these fertilizers at some distance from the root, using a single barrowful of mellow, rather rich soil, to add to the earth in which to plant the tree.

CHAPTER III.

METHODS OF PROPAGATION AND IMPROVEMENT OF KINDS.

The mode of propagating fruit trees more practised than any other is grafting or budding good kinds on young stocks.

The stocks, or young ungrafted wild trees, are trees which have sprung from seed, suckers springing from the roots of old trees, layers or cuttings. The last two are more difficult to obtain, but if taken from a tree above the graft, their fruit will be of the cultivated kind. It is only when the layer or cutting is laid or taken below the graft, that it will be a stock requiring working or grafting.

The grafts do not entirely overbear the nature of the stock, so that a graft of a kind characterized by fine foliage and vigorous growth, should be used on a stock of similar nature, and *vice versâ*. A slight difference, however, is beneficial in increasing fertility. If stock and graft be too unlike in vigour of growth, temporary success may result, but not the production of good lasting trees. The stock, too, as a general rule, should be of rather earlier vegetation than the scion. The size at which the young stocks may be grafted or budded is the time the stem measures from a quarter of an inch to one inch in diameter, but stems or branches two or three inches or more in diameter are sometimes worked with success.

Mature trees, that produce inferior fruit, do very well for pruning quite close and grafting again, provided they are in health and vigour of growth, but old, unhealthy, worn-out trees are not worth doing: it is better to root up such and plant young trees in their place.

Crab stocks are wild fruit trees, their seedlings or suckers, such as the wild crab apple of our hedges, wild pears, wild plums, wild cherries, or in fact the produce of any trees which have not been grafted. They throw their roots deep into the earth, and produce trees which are fitter for orchard than for garden culture.

Free stocks are produced from seed or layers of cultivated fruit. They partake in some measure of the character of the parent tree, and if the natural fruit be waited for it may prove new or good, but it is generally many years before it comes.

Paradise, or *Doucin stocks* are layers or suckers from a dwarf kind of apple, which keeps the roots much nearer the surface than *crab stocks*, and which is consequently much easier to cultivate, manure, and keep in lasting vigour. The *French Paradise* stock is distinguished by very dwarf growth, clear brown shoots, and fibrous roots spreading near the surface of the ground. The so-called *English Paradise* is said to be intermediate in habit between the very dwarf habit of the French, and the rampant growth of the crab. French cultivators make a distinction between the *Doucin* and *Pomme de Paradis*, naming the Doucin stocks as good for pyramidal pruned trees, and the Pomme de Paradis for dwarf trees.

Quince stocks, or young trees grown from the Quince, are excellent for pears in producing the compact, dwarfed habit of growth so favourable for keeping that delicious fruit in perfect garden cultivation, and safe from the late frost and tearing wind which so often, between them, bring our pear crops to nil.

The *Mahaleb stock, cerasus Mahaleb*, or perfumed cherry, is a stock which is good for dwarf cherries, and the wild stock does for making tall orchard trees. It is called the perfumed cherry on account of the pleasant scent of the wood when it is burned, and it is named *bois de St. Lucia* in France; it has long been used as stocks for cherries, and it will do in more ordinary soils than will suit common cherry stocks. It may be obtained from the Mahaleb by layers or cuttings. Cherry stocks grown from the kernel may be sown in February, the stones having been kept in sand till then, planted out in October, and budded the next season for dwarf trees, or allowed to grow tall if they are wanted for standards.

Apples are grafted on crab or Doucin stocks: the first for large, the other for dwarf growth. They are also grafted on the white thorn. Pears for dwarf and easy garden culture, are grafted on the Quince stock, and those of a larger growth on free stocks. Almonds are budded on seedling plum stocks. Apricots may be budded on apricot or plum stocks, and a wild plum is used with advantage. Peaches and nectarines may be budded on almond stocks peach stocks, raised from the stone, or the muscle plum: the last is best in our climate. Plums are grafted or budded on the muscle stock, or on the Brussels stock. Cherries on the Mahaleb and wild stock. For all trees which are apt to exhaust themselves by the exudation of gum, budding is preferable to grafting. Medlars may be grafted on a white thorn or on a pear.

Figs, vines, gooseberries, and currants are not grafted, but are increased by cuttings or layers. Raspberries and strawberries may be grown from seed, but are generally increased, the first by dividing of the suckers, the last by the runners.

Raising plants from seed is a method of propagation requiring great care and skill, and often leading to the production of choice new varieties. The seed chosen may be either itself of the choicest kind, or scientifically improved by crossing two fine sorts. If it be wished to raise trees or plants of one particular variety, not only should the best tree be chosen, but the finest fruit, ripened under the most favourable circumstances, must also be selected. However fine the old tree from which seed is taken, the seedlings from it will not do it credit, unless it be grown in a genial position, and unless its fruit, the germ of the future seedlings, be grown to high perfection, under genial influences, and brought to full maturity in size, ripeness, and development of juice, flavour, and saccharine matter. To give a good chance of success with seedlings, therefore, raise them from the finest fruit, plucked from the finest tree, and ripened and brought to perfection under the most favourable circumstances possible.

Cross fertilization, or setting the flower of one tree with the pollen from the flower of another, is a valuable way of improving kinds. It is generally only varieties of the same fruit which can be thus crossed, but valuable qualities are often united by it. In this crossing the offspring will most resemble the stock from which the pollen is taken, but will also follow some of the constitutional peculiarities of that producing the seed. That fine plum, Coe's golden drop, was grown from a greengage, the flower of which had been set with pollen from the yellow Magnum Bonum: the Grafton cherry, set with pollen from the white-heart, produced the Elton cherry. Varieties thus crossed are sometimes more productive than either parent, and their produce is susceptible of improvement by careful culture.

Growing from eyes is a simple mode of propagation, now much used for making vines, and for some other purposes. A single eye, a leaf bud, is extracted from a plant, and planted with due allowance of heat and moisture, and in time it too becomes a plant.

Striking cuttings is an easy method of propagation in the case of all plants which strike easily. Some hardy fruit trees will throw out roots tolerably readily. The cuttings must each possess several leaf buds, and be planted with one or two below the ground, the others above it. The lowest bud will soon throw out root, and imbibe nourishment from the earth, while those above ground, developing their leaves, will draw up nourishment, until in time the cutting becomes a plant or tree. The end of October is the time for taking cuttings, if the tree have lost its leaves by then, but any time from the fall of the leaf to the first swelling of the buds in spring will do; for callus, the matter exuding from the edges of a wound in a plant during the process of healing, through which in cuttings the roots and perpendicular vessels connected with them proceed, forms at the lower end even during winter. The situation in which the cuttings are planted should be neither sunny and dry, nor too shady, as that would make them run up weak. The north side of a wall, not less than four feet from it, is a good position: here they will be in shade during the spring, while they are rooting, and by about midsummer, when all that take will be well established, they will thrive in the sunshine which they will then get. Plant the cuttings rather firm at their lower ends, and if very dry weather occur in March, April, or May, give them a sprinkling of water now and then.

A way of planting cuttings of fruit trees was described in the *Cottage Gardener* a few years back, by means of which I have seen kinds of fruit trees saved which I should have been sorry to have lost. In such a locality as that above described, and in October, as soon as the leaves are down, make two shallow parallel trenches, one foot apart, and raise the earth thrown out upon the ridge between them. From the fruit trees which are to be propagated, cut straight twigs a foot and a half long, taking especial care to leave the ends uncut. Plant the two ends of each cutting, one in each trench, arching the centre over the ridge, close down upon it, cover all with earth except the centre bud, and it will in time throw out roots and leaves, and become a little tree by the following summer.

Laying or layering is growing cuttings without severing the connection between them and the parent tree until after the root is formed. To facilitate the growth of root, the layers are often tongued, *i.e.*, the stem to be layered is partly cut through, close to a bud, when the roots will push into the earth more easily than they would make their way through the firm bark. The layers are partly covered with earth, the ends being left out, firmly pegged down, allowed to root from the underground portion, and, when well grown, separated from the parent tree or plant.

Sprays of plants may be rooted in pots, while still growing on the tree. Pass a shoot through the bole in a garden pot, giving it a slight cut or twist by the bud nearest the bottom of the pot or not, according to the nature of the plant for rooting readily or the contrary, fill the pot with mould or compost, and the spray, if rooted and grown, may be separated the following autumn. This is good for wood which will not bear bending.

CHAPTER IV

GRAFTING AND BUDDING.

IN the method of multiplying the trees of one variety without change of character, so well known as grafting, *i.e.*, uniting a scion, or producing shoot, of one plant to the root, branch, or stem of another, for it to grow and take life from the root, the scion and stock must be of nearly related species.

The uses of grafting are many. By it trees of a desired kind may be multiplied to almost any extent. Those of too puny or too rampant a habit, may be adjusted by grafting on a stock of greater or less vigour of growth than the tree itself. When seedling trees are grafted, it accelerates their productiveness; shoots from seedlings will be hastened into bearing by being grafted on stocks, and kinds may be adapted to soils in which they would not do well on their own roots, by being grafted on stocks suited to the locality. Lastly, old kinds may be renovated, renewed, and saved from annihilation, to some extent, by grafts.

The nature of the stock does not change that of the fruit of the scion; it only conveys nourishment to it, so that it may alter it in productiveness, and in some degree in size, but not in form, flavour, or other properties more intimately belonging to the kind.

To facilitate the rising of the sap, the stock should be in rather a forwarder state of growth than the graft. If the parent tree and the stock be in an equal state of forwardness, it is best to cut the grafts, and stick their ends into the earth in a cool, shady spot, and leave them for a certain number of days, or even for some weeks. The operation should be performed neatly and promptly, and none but a keen, clean knife used, for dirt or a ragged cut is likely to prevent success. Both stock and scion should be in a thoroughly healthy condition. Never cut for a scion an unhealthy-looking twig, or one which is faulty in the bark, but choose fine, healthy, well-ripened shoots of the preceding year's growth.

There are several different kinds of grafting, but whatever the kind, the manipulation is similar in all important points. The stock for almost all grafting is topped back to the proper height, it and the scion cleanly cut to fit each other, the scion or graft accurately adjusted and tied on with firmness and precision, from a little below to a little above the union, taking care that the tie be tight enough to keep the graft immovable, but not tight enough to cause any danger of its cutting or bruising the bark.

For tying the graft, wide strands of bass, or bast, used to be best liked, but now soft cotton is found to answer better, and worsted is better still.

When the graft is affixed and tied on, the tie is surrounded with clay worked into a tenacious dough, to exclude the air and keep the part intended to adhere moist.

To make grafting clay, beat some horse droppings to pieces, and pass them through a half-inch riddle, mix this well with equal parts of clayey loam and fresh cow manure, add a little road drift, and knead all together into a pliant dough of uniform consistence. Shape this in a spindle-shaped lump over the spot where the graft is fixed on, and smooth the outside with the hand dipped in fine ashes, which enables the grafter to close the surface perfectly. Look over the grafts a few days after they are put in, and if the clay show cracks anywhere, they should be closed, and the surface made smooth again.

Clayey loam or brick earth, well beaten with a fourth part of fresh, sheer cow dung, and a little hay cut into pieces an inch long to bind it, makes a good grafting clay, and many gardeners use moist clay alone, or a little cow manure plastered over the graft, and covered with moss or coarse brown paper, tied on.

Grafting wax, for the same purpose as the grafting clay, is made by melting in a pipkin over the fire half an ounce of wax and half an ounce of fat; half an ounce of red sealing-wax is broken in pieces and put into this, and the whole is kept stirred until all are thoroughly melted and mixed together; a very little honey is stirred in at last, and the mixture is poured into moulds, and still stirred gently until it begins to set.

Another grafting wax is made by melting together bees' wax, pitch, tallow, and a little bit of resin.

To use the grafting wax, make it warm enough to be laid on the graft with a brush, paint it on until it is a quarter of an inch thick, and then dust a little dry sand all over the surface, to prevent its melting.

The spring is the season for grafting. The time should be chosen when the sap is just rising in the stock, and before the buds in the scion begin to swell. Promptitude is as necessary as precision—a dawdling grafter or budder is very seldom a successful one. The weather favourable to the operation is that which is mild and moist; a drying east wind is fatal to success, and cold weather is bad, whether it be dry or wet. Some persons encourage the sap to rise by covering the earth round the roots with litter, rotten tan, or decayed leaves, and others even water with warm water after the grafting.

It is necessary that the inner bark of stock and scion be intimately united. This union is sometimes of the bark all round, as is generally the case with whip-grafting, and sometimes only on one side, as in side-grafting.

Whip or splice-grafting is that in most use for fruit trees. It is best for the stock and scion to be the same size in diameter, as then the union of the two takes place all round, and is very secure; but this is not imperative, as the scion will grow if the inner bark or alburnum in stock and scion intimately join in one part only. Prune off the stock to the desired height. The graft should have at least three or four buds. Trim the graft by cutting it with a long, diagonal cut, nearly, but not quite through, and finish the operation with a short cut, to meet the long cut at an angle. This second cut, making a kind of notch, fixes the graft much more firmly than when formed with one cut sloping all the way. The stock must be cut with a tongue to fit the notch in the graft as exactly as possible, stock and graft accurately placed inner bark to inner bark, and bound round and round securely with soft cotton, or strips of bass.

If the stock be larger round than the graft, the portion of the graft left by the *long cut* must be adjusted to the outer side of the stock, the notch being inward. This inequality in size of stock and graft is often unavoidable, especially in grafting old trees. In grafting young on old, allowance must be made for the greater thickness and roughness of the outer bark on the old tree, as compared with the younger bark on the graft.

Crown or wedge-grafting is sometimes used for fruit trees. The graft is shaped into a wedge of rather a sharp angle, with two equal slanting cuts, a cleft to correspond is cut in the stock, and the graft fixed as in whip-grafting. If stock and graft do not agree in size, bark must fit to bark on *one* side. Vines are grafted in this manner. In their case, some growing portion must be left on the stock above the graft, to draw up the sap and prevent bleeding.

Cleft-grafting is a kind of crown-grafting which is often found convenient for stocks of large size, for if they are an inch or more in diameter, whip-grafting will not do well in their case. Cut or saw off the head of the stock, pare the bottom of the graft into a wedge an inch and a half long, make a cleft in the stock, with a strong knife or cutting chisel, about two inches deep, leaving the chisel in to keep it open. Insert the graft, adjusting the thin end of the wedge in the bottom of the cleft, with bark to bark. remove the chisel, and the cleft will hold the graft firm. Tie it and cover it with clay. If the stock be large enough, a second graft may be inserted at the other end of the cleft, opposite the first; and I have known three or four different sorts of apples grafted on an apple tree several years old, which did not bear, and all do well.

Saddle-grafting is like crown-grafting reversed: the stock is shaped into a wedge, the cleft is made in the graft, which is placed over the wedge, like a saddle. As in all grafting, bark and bark must meet, at any rate on one side, and the tying is the same.

A peculiar kind of saddle-grafting is practised in the apple-growing counties, sometimes even in the middle of summer. The stock is larger than the graft, which is slit up about four inches, one-third from one side.

The stock is cut off in a slanting direction; the outer bark is then cut through in a vertical line from the centre of the highest point, the slit a little opened, and the stoutest cut of the graft inserted, inner bark to inner bark. The thinner strip of the graft is carried over to the other side of the stock, and in like manner inserted in a long vertical opening; when the graft is tied in the usual way.

Side-grafting is sometimes useful to provide against the falling off of old trees, to utilize a healthy trunk of a poor bearing sort, or in case of scarcity of stocks. A downward, slightly slanting cut is made on one side of the stem of the tree. The graft is slit up, and each division pared off to a thin edge, one side is inserted in the cleft and the other bound outside. For side-grafting of smaller shoots, cut a slice downwards on one side of the stock, and remove this shave down with a horizontal cut, shave off a bit of the stock, cut it straight at the bottom to fit, and fit it and fasten it on. This grafting may sometimes be found advantageous, as the head of the stock being left on, draws up the sap. It is sometimes done by merely shaving off a strip from the stock, and the same from the graft, adjusting and tying them, and then placing the lower end of the graft in a vial of water.

Shoulder or chink-grafting is as the name describes it; both stock and graft are cut in a zigzag, which of course offers more surface of alburnum to unite. The stock and graft must agree in size.

For root-grafting, or grafting on the root, sometimes practised to utilize large scions, this zigzag cut is used. Neither that nor peg-grafting (for which the graft is cut in the form of a peg to fit into a receptacle made in the stock) is much used for fruit trees.

Inarching, a plan for making the graft take and grow before it is severed from the parent tree, can only be used with close neighbours or plants in pots. Where it is practicable, it is excellent for all kinds that take badly. Tie together the branches that will unite without strain, and mark on both the spot which is best for the union. Then in both the stock and in the branch to be attached, pare away the bark with a little of the wood to it in strips two or three inches long; those on stock and graft to agree. Make a slit upwards in the branch, so as to form a kind of tongue, and a slit downwards in the stock. Unite the two, slipping the tongue in the graft into the slit in the stock: take care that the inner barks touch, and tie them firmly with cotton or bass. Each graft should be supported by a stake, or the rugging of the wind may loosen them. Inarching, like other grafting, is performed in the spring; in about four months the graft may be cut from the parent tree, with great care and delicacy not to disturb the adhesion. The stock may then, too, be headed back to near the graft, and the clay and bandages removed, and replaced with new ones, to remain a fortnight or three weeks longer. If the union be not found to be perfect, at the end of four months or so, the new bandages had better be kept on for another year, and the graft still left for that time attached to the parent tree. This kind of grafting is used for vines, orange trees, camelias, and similar plants.

After whip-grafting and the other most usual methods, the clay may be removed and the ties loosened, when the graft has made shoots a few inches long, but care must be taken not to disturb them prematurely. In the open air, all the ties may generally be finally removed in August; and if the grafted plants have been kept in-doors, rather earlier; but windy weather should be avoided for the purpose, to prevent accidents.

Budding (or grafting by growing a portion from one tree on a stock from a bud instead of from a scion) is often used with fruit trees, especially in the case of those which are apt to bleed or exude gum from cuts in the wood. It has the same uses and advantages as other kinds of grafting.

Buds are said to be two years later than grafts in producing fruit, but where grafts are difficult to get, they have the advantage that a single bud will suffice, whereas a graft must have three or four. Buds from seedling peaches and pears, will bear earlier than the parent trees, and produce finer fruit, if they are inserted on robust stocks in a similar though inferior manner to scions so used; but if pears are budded before the end of August, they will produce branches and no bloom. It is not necessary that the inserted bud should take the position of a bud removed, but some persons consider that it does better so placed. A bud will often take more readily than a graft, and it has another advantage: if a graft fails in the spring, the bud may be inserted at its right time, and so save a year.

Buds take well on shoots of one or two years' growth, but not on old wood. The time for budding is July or August, according to the season, and the weather should be mild and moist. Early in the morning, after 3 P.M., or in the evening of a cloudy day, after gentle rain, and when there is no wind, is best. The stock may be smaller than for grafting, and it is rather best to put the bud on the north side, but it must be on a clear portion of the stem, free from knots. It is necessary that the stock should be in a thriving state, *i. e.*, sufficiently supplied with sap, and should have matured its growth for the season, which generally happens in peaches, apricots, cherries, and plums, about the middle of August; but from the middle of July, favourable states of stocks and buds, and favourable states of weather, should be carefully watched and taken advantage of. Watering the stock and the tree from which the buds are to be taken the evening before, will generally do good.

The bud should be from wood of the current year: that to be taken for budding is the little bud which pushes at the axis of the leaf-stalk, and it is cleanly cut with a small oval shield of the bark of the stem behind, and this shield is cut deep enough to include a thin shave of the wood. Choose one at the root of a well-developed, faultless leaf. The buds are ready when the bark will easily separate from the wood, and one from about the middle of a shoot should be fixed on, as those near the base take less readily, and those from the end are said to make too much wood. If the bark will not rise, *i. e.*, will not part freely from the wood, the bud will not take.

Dexterity and quickness are absolutely necessary in budding, as the bark and bud must not have time to dry before the operation is completed. Therefore have ready all that will be necessary before beginning. A budding-knife is the usual and best tool, but any good sharp knife will do: some bass cut and divided into pieces of convenient length and width, or else worsted or cotton in lengths, and the twigs with the buds, divested of leaves and placed in water, must all be at hand.

Before cutting the bud, prepare the incision ready to receive it. Determine the exact spot where the bud is to go, and cut a horizontal incision of sufficient length to admit the shield attached to the bud, about the third of an inch in length, a little more or a little less, according to the size of the bud. Then make a perpendicular cut to meet the centre of this, beginning half an inch (more or less) below the horizontal cut, and cutting upwards to meet it at a right angle. The whole incision will then have the form of a **T**, and should be deep enough to go just down to the wood. Some persons wrap a bit of something wet round it. Cut the bud with a small oval slice of the bark and wood to it. If the bud is very backward, do not disturb the small shave of wood behind it, but if it be pretty well formed this may be carefully removed with the point of the knife. The root of the bud behind the shield should look plump.

Cut and prepare the bud as quickly as possible, raise the bark on the stock a little down each side of the longitudinal cut in the **T**-shaped incision with the thin end of the budding-knife, if one be used, and then slip the little shield of the bud in at the cross cut, and downwards under the bark to the bottom of the **T**; cut off the top of the shield to fit the top of the **T**, and tie the bud in pretty firmly with wet bass or worsted, beginning with a turn just above the bud, working to a little below the incision, and upwards to a little above it. The leaf-stalk should be left to the bud to hold it by.

In unfavourable seasons a watering with liquid manure at a temperature of 90° may be given to the parent tree the day before, to make the sap rise.

When the bud is fixed, tie a leaf from an evergreen by each end, to arch over the newly inserted bud, to shade it.

In a few weeks the buds should be looked at, and the ties loosened if they seem too tight; and they may be removed when the bud has firmly grown into the stock.

For niche-budding the bud is cut with a stouter shield, which is cut straight at the bottom. A notch is then made in the stock, round at the top and flat at the bottom, for the shield to fit into exactly, and in adjusting it care is taken to unite the inner bark of stock and shield. As it is the inner bark which grows, as in grafting, this is rather on the principle of grafting than of budding, in which it is the bud which throws its fibres into the stock. Some persons consider that for this budding a spot should be chosen in the stock where a bud is removed.

Annular budding is similar in character. The branch from which the bud is taken must be as thick as the stock; if a little thicker it is of no consequence. A ring of bark with a bud on it, opened at one side to let it off, is taken, a ring like it is removed from the stock, and the ring with the bud put on and tied. It is considered to answer very well with thick-barked trees.

Beginners in grafting and budding would do well to get the opportunity of watching the process under the hands of dexterous operators, and having once seen it, written instructions can be much more readily followed.

CHAPTER V.

CULTURE OF FRUIT TREES.—PRUNING.

The fruit of the wild stock and of our cultivated trees, differing from each other as the aborigines of Australia and the best-educated natives of London, are yet scarcely more dissimilar than the produce of a tree which is just grafted or budded and then left to chance, and that of one kept in a high state of cultivation by pruning, training, manuring, and all the attention necessary to bring it into first-rate order in the flavour and size of its fruit. It is as unfair to leave a fruit tree to nature and expect good fruit from it, as to leave a child uneducated and look for fine sentiments and learning in the adult.

Flavour in fruit is very dependent on a healthy development of the leaves, which again depends on air and light, as much as on the nourishment derived from the earth, so that clear, pure air is favourable to the production of good fruit, and there are few kinds which will thrive in a smoke-laden atmosphere.

Manuring is often necessary to keep up the stamina of the trees, but it must be administered with caution, or it may only produce a rampant growth of foliage and wood instead of fruit. When trees are planted the earth should be made tolerably rich with manure of a good lasting kind, as already mentioned, and that afterwards given must be so used as to encourage the roots to keep near the surface of the ground. A little mulching or spreading a layer of litter on the surface round the tree (to be afterwards lightly forked in in winter) may sometimes do good when the fruit is swelling.

The most important items of cultivation, after good air and good soil, are pruning and training.

Pruning is necessary to increase the productiveness of all fruit-bearing trees, since a too rampant growth precludes fruitfulness. Nature impels a tree to vigorous growth of foliage and wood, and little production of fruit, the result of free, unchecked circulation of the sap: art, by checking the free circulation of the sap, by pruning and training, forces the tree to bear bloom instead of leaf-buds only. This is the principle on which we prune our trees.

The object of pruning is so to regulate the branches as to encourage bloom and the full development of the fruit, without too much curtailing the leaf surface, in which the circulation of the juices takes place, and different kinds of pruning are applicable to different fruit trees.

In pruning, the productiveness of the tree in hand, and its beauty, must both be made matters of consideration. Every tree is a study in itself, and every cut with the pruning-knife must be matter of calculation, and be made for some reason regarding present or future growth and productiveness, or the just balance necessary to form a handsome tree.

Most kinds of trees require summer and winter pruning. For summer pruning much labour and loss of sap may be saved by rubbing off the buds or nipping off tiny shoots which are going to produce branches that would have to be removed afterwards. This prevention of evil should be constantly attended to throughout the growing season. The object of summer pruning is to mature the fruit, and improve the beauty of the tree: it may be begun in May. Trees of a naturally rampant growth should be allowed to retain more main branches than those of a more puny habit, to give play to the too abundant sap; and as growth proceeds, shoots which are or will be wanted must be trained in from time to time, to prevent their starting from their place and taking a wrong direction.

The winter pruning is to regulate the main branches and the young wood of the past summer, and the time for it is open weather, from the fall of the leaf until the sap begins to rise in spring; but it had better be done in good time. The trained trees which require new wood every year,—such as peaches, nectarines, apricots, and vines, must be taken down from the wall for the main pruning.

The mode of bearing of different sorts of trees must be considered before cutting them.

Apples, pears, plums, and cherries bear on spurs, or short, robust side-shoots from half an inch to one or two inches long, growing from wood of from two to twenty years old. The same branches bear year after year, so that when these trees are trained to a good head, no more wood is wanted than any that may occasionally be required to train up to supply the place of unproductive or dead branches. Constant nipping back is therefore the most important pruning they require.

In summer, to throw the strength into the bearing spurs, all the shoots should be cut back, except leading shoots, which are necessary to draw up the sap; and in winter, all the branches should be so radically thinned out where necessary as to let in plenty of air and light to the heart of the tree, the leading shoots left in summer being shortened first.

Peaches, nectarines, and apricots produce their fruit on one-year old wood; thus that which grows this year produces next. In pruning these trees, therefore, the object to be kept in view is to leave a good supply of the finest young wood on fairly-grown shoots at regular distances, at every side, from the bottom of the tree to its extremities. In their summer pruning, rub off the leaf-buds which would produce crowded or cross-growing branches, and leave the rest. In winter, shorten the old wood, less or more, according to its strength, to make it throw out young wood in proper positions the following year, and train in the summer-grown shoots.

Vines bear on wood of the same year, shooting from eyes on one-year old wood. Train in a sufficiency of shoots of the current year for producing the next year, and in winter shorten them to a few eyes each, to shoot and bear the following season.

Figs bear on one-year old wood, which must not be shortened, as the fruit comes on the ends; but the tree should be judiciously thinned out in its non-active season, and superfluous thickness may be prevented by disbudding, *i. e.*, by rubbing off leaf-buds wherever they are too thick.

Filberts produce on one-year old wood, and the pruner must use his knife to encourage its production by shortening back robust sprays, to make them throw out laterally, and this may be done early in February, when the blossom shows, and cutting it away can be avoided.

One main object to be kept in view in pruning is to let in air and light abundantly to the fruit in summer, and to all the branches and to the heart of the tree at all seasons. Winter pruning should not be done so early that the tree will shoot again, but in trees that produce from spurs it may, under particular circumstances, take place before vegetation ceases, when the impetus given to the shortened branch will cause spurs to form. In every branch pruned consider the future, as in every tree that is cut peculiar circumstances will occur which can only be judged of on the spot, and at the time. Practice and observation patiently carried on can alone effect skill in pruning fruit trees.

The knife for pruning should be sharp and clean, to make a neat, clean cut, which as a general rule should be on a slant, in woody stems, that the rain may run off. All dead branches should be neatly removed, and for this purpose a saw will often be required. When the branch is partly sawed through from the upper surface, make a cut with the saw a short distance, to meet the first, from the under side, and when the branch is nearly sawed through, let it be held or tied with care, to support its weight, and to prevent a splintering breakage at last. A splintered break in sawing a tree is a great eyesore, besides being injurious to the tree in letting moisture sop into the wood.

It is often the fate of cultivators to have to take in hand and make the best of gardens of long standing, full of moss-grown, ill-used, cumbrous old trees, crowded with dead branches and unproductive wood. These trees are too old and un-get-at-able to be brought to order by any common treatment, but they need not therefore be despised and rooted up untried, for excellent old sorts are often hidden in their ungainly growth, and may be brought forth to show themselves with a little care, whereas it would take years to supply their place with young trees in good bearing. Leave such trees in their unsightly ugliness until the fall of the leaf. In the meantime taste the fruit, if any opportunity for so doing be given, to ascertain if it have capabilities.

When leaves and sap are down, take saw and pruning-knife in hand, and have no mercy on the old trees, but cut away most liberally, yet judiciously, of course. First remove all the dead wood, sawing off the dead or dying branches down to the trunk with a smooth, clean cut, and if the white round left be an eyesore, it can be rubbed over with a little dark earth, rubbed up with cow manure. After this, thin out the branches well, leaving the middle of the tree quite open, and every branch divided from its neighbours by space enough to let in plenty of air, light, and sun, and prune the remaining branches in the right way, according to the kind. Get a scrubbing-brush, soft or other soap, and plenty of water, and scrub all the bark of the trees, trunk and branches, as far as can be got at, thoroughly clean of moss, lichen, dirt, and insects. If the trees be very much reduced, a mulching of manure, to soak in with winter rains, may do good.

Destruction, root and branch, is often recommended by gardeners, but this careful reformatory treatment of the old trees, with little more trouble and less expense than planting new ones, will often prove much more satisfactory in the look of the garden and in the fruit crop. As I said before, old fruit trees of fine sorts are not to be despised.

CHAPTER VI.

CULTURE OF FRUIT TREES.—TRAINING.

Pruning and training go hand in hand. The knife in the hand of the foreseeing pruner removes all that would spread into unsightly growth, and spares the buds and branches likely to grow in a direction to form the tree to productiveness, uniformity, and beauty. Thus the pruner does half the trainer's work, and leaves him little but the finishing up with the hammer and nails. As an education with a good foundation may finish itself, so a tree well cut will shape itself: the pruner's work is all-important, although that of the trainer makes a good continuation. In speaking of the culture of fruit trees, however, we cannot separate pruning and training, since pruning very often is training (or reducing to shape, order, and productiveness) prophetically.

Training, or regulating the position of the branches in fruit trees, has for its object both the free admission of light and air, and encouraging productiveness by turning the shoots aside from their upward growth. Indifferent bearers will often be brought to bear well by merely bending the branches downwards, or to a right angle with the stem of the tree. The motion of the branches in the wind, and their upward growth, encourage free circulation of sap, whereas the development of fruit requires its retention in the bearing branches. On this account productiveness is often created or improved by bending branches downwards, and on this principle, also (as well as from the warmth retained by a wall), training trees on walls or espaliers is advantageous.

A tree intended for training should be reduced to the necessary order very early in life, by pruning it so that it may have only a few branches well placed for training into a fan-like shape. For espaliers, trees of similar growth must be chosen to those intended for training on walls. As a border to the paths in fruit gardens, they take less room than standards, and so are sometimes valuable in small gardens. The training, too, encourages productiveness and keeps them conveniently within reach for culture and for gathering the fruit. Iron hurdles are used by some cultivators for training-espaliers. They may be bought six feet long, and three feet high, with five bars, and weighing about 36 lbs. each, for 4s. 6d. each; those of stronger make would of course be more in proportion. Wooden ones, although less lasting, may be made tolerably permanent by fixing upright stakes, to remain, of oak or larch. These should be as near each other as two or three feet apart, and horizontal bars of a less lasting and less expensive kind can be used, and renewed when necessary. A few intermediate uprights may be wanted just until the trees gain stability.

Table trellises are trellises fixed horizontally about half a yard from the ground. Arched trellis, a kind of arcade of wire, for training trees over, and some for single trees, in form like an umbrella, are fanciful and pretty.

Good trellises for currants may be made very simply of stout laths fixed in a large trellis pattern, meeting or crossing only at the top, bottom, and in the middle; they are very convenient for covering the trees to preserve the fruit. Standard trees are those, as their name implies, which are grown to stand out without support from wall or trellis. Full standards are up-growing tall trees, generally several feet high in the trunk, before the branches divide to form a head. Half standards are standards the trunks of which are only two or three feet high before the spreading of the head. Dwarf standards are trees which are of a dwarf habit of growth, and they are by far the most advantageous kind for garden culture, as they are quite within reach, for the best culture, and for gathering the fruit. The dwarf habit depends on the stock used. Dwarf standards are kept in form by judicious pruning, and can easily be kept so open in the centre that the sun and air have full influence over the tree and its fruit.

Quenouille training, or training with one centre stem in such a manner that the whole tree has the shape of a spindle, small at the stem (of course), bulging out in the middle, and coming again to a point at the top, is good for dwarf trees, and has been very fashionable with some Belgian and English pear-growers. The young tree from the first is trained to one central stem, which is shortened back to fifteen inches high for its winter pruning; this will make it throw out laterally.

The side-shoots are trained horizontally, and the shoot produced from the highest bud is made to grow as straight upright as possible, during the summer, and then cut back so far as to make it shoot fifteen inches above the first round of shoots. The same process is continued until the tree is as high as it is wished to be. To make the side-shoots take the horizontal growth required for *quenouille* training, fix little stakes round the tree, tie the lowest range of shoots to them in a horizontal direction, and then train each succeeding range to the one below, to give all the same horizontal growth. The shoots thus arched downwards will soon bear, and they must be pruned to produce fruit-spurs like other trees; but care must be taken in the pruning not to cut the shoots so short as to induce them to make a too crowded growth. Trees trained *à la quenouille* require more constant care and watching than usually trained dwarf trees, or they lose the peculiar form and become too bushy. The pear must be on the quince stock.

Balloon training is curious, and peculiar. A standard of slender growth is chosen, and all the branches are trained over downwards towards the ground.

Pyramidal training is more popular than *quenouille* training; and it has the advantages of beauty of growth, of keeping the trees within a manageable size, easy of culture, and safe from storms, and of leaving the surrounding garden-ground unshaded and available for other crops. It will do for pears on quince stocks, apples on paradise stocks, cherries on Mahaleb stocks, and for plums, and it will produce finer fruit on a smaller area of ground than any other mode of culture.

To produce a perfect pyramid, the little tree should be taken in training the year after it is grafted, and it should be one of a nice straight growth, with a fair supply of buds, from the insertion of the graft upwards. As in the *quenouille* training, head it down to fifteen inches high, or rather taller, let it branch at the sides, and train the top shoot into a leader, as upright as possible. When this leading shoot is ten inches long, nip off the top; it will produce side-shoots, which must be a little trained into form if necessary, and the top bud (if there are two or more, rub off all but one) may again be trained straight up for a leader. Early in September shorten all the shoots to six or seven buds, and take care to lead them out from the main stem by a little judicious training, that the young tree may not acquire too thick and cluttered a growth. The second year of training, the topped side-shoots will put forth plentifully; when all these young shoots have put forth several leaves, their tops must be nipped off. This will be about June or July, according to the season and locality, and if these spurs shoot, the young shoots must be nipped back to one leaf, but the leading shoot of each side branch must be left to grow until August, to draw up the sap, and to prevent the tree's exhausting itself by a too abundant side growth. In August these may also be cut back.

If the buds so tend to one side as to leave the pyramid irregular in growth, buds may be budded into the bare places, but only bad culture can render this necessary.

The shoots left by the June nipping back will be productive fruit-spurs the following year, and the pruning can best be done with a pair of rose scissors. As the tree grows older the same system of pruning is followed. The leading shoots left intact until August prevents too thick a growth of shoots, and the shoots nipped back in summer form fruit-bearing spurs the following season. After the shortening of leading shoots in August, no winter pruning is required.

The same system of pruning and training, *i. e.*, continually nipping back all the shoots, except the leading shoots, through the summer, leaving the leading shoots until the sap begins to descend, and then shortening them, succeeds well with any dwarf trees, and produces most abundant crops of fruit under almost any circumstances. In dwarf trees grown as bushes, winter thinning out of any branches that become too crowded is often necessary.

In the August shortening of leaders, pear trees of very vigorous growth, such as Beurré d'Amaulis, Monsieur le Curé, Bucrré Diel, and others, should have them shortened back to eight or ten inches; pears of medium vigour, such as Louise Bonne, Marie Louise, Buerré d'Aremberg, and such like, shortened to six inches; and pears of puny growth, like Winter Nelis, to only four inches, because the abundant sap of the rampant growers will expend itself in a too crowded growth, if necessary scope be not allowed. Difference of soil, difference in habit of trees, even of the same kind, situation, and many other circumstances, will often make a considerable difference in the vigorous growth of particular trees.

Cordon training, so much spoken of during the last few years, is a name introduced by French fruit-growers for the system which is the very soul of good fruit culture, pinching in all the shoots, to form a succession of flower-buds. The ends of all the shoots on a branch are pinched off, and thus made to produce bloom, so that each tree or each branch is kept to a single, unbranching stem.

In cordon training, the whole tree is sometimes kept to a single stem. These trees are planted very close together against a wall, and are trained diagonally, at an angle of about 45°, all the trees being kept parallel with each other. Another mode is to train the branches in this manner, all starting from one upright centre stem.

For vertical cordon training a young tree with a centre and two side branches is chosen, the centre branch is trained straight upright on the wall, and the side branches are trained horizontally, and their side branches again vertically, in parallel lines with the main stem. The pruning and management is like that of pyramidal trained trees, and the save of room will be found to be great. The vertical branches from the side branches may be trained eight inches from each other, as they are not to be allowed to branch at the sides.

The diagonal cordon training is best for peaches, but the vertical cordon system does well for pears, cherries on the Mahaleb stock, plums and apples on the paradise stock.

Cordon training on table trellises set on a slope, and covered with glazed frames, while the trees are in flower, and while the fruit swells, does well for apricots, peaches, and nectarines, and the necessary apparatus for such frames is less costly than the orchard-house, and much more portable. The radiation of heat from the earth makes the fruit very fine, and the same plan produces pears in great perfection. The lights should be taken off in July, and the fruit from that time left exposed to sun and air. In cold localities the frames may be left on a month later.

Pears on the quince stock sometimes will not flourish on warm, shallow soils with chalk or gravel beneath. Pyramids on pear stocks will make better trees for such localities. A young grafted tree should be taken in hand, and treated and trained as the pyramid on the quince stock, mentioned some pages back.

Root-pruning is had recourse to for the purpose of checking the over-luxuriance of trees, and thus not only keeping them to a manageable size, but creating productiveness by checking a too luxuriant growth.

Abundance of sap, and its free, unimpeded circulation, tends to the growth of leaf-buds, and consequently to a vigorous increase of branches, whereas impeding the circulation of the sap causes fruit-buds to form in place of the more exuberant leaf-buds. I have known a young apple tree forced into premature productiveness by careless neglect of removing the ligatures that tied the graft. Root-pruning beneficially impedes a too luxuriant growth by diminishing the quantity of sap in the tree, from diminishing the quantity of food with which it is supplied. It is especially good for rendering a tree productive which is barren from an over-luxuriant growth, *i. e.*, from all the strength of the tree running to leaf, and for retaining a dwarf habit of growth, so suitable for keeping trees within due limits for easy culture, and well adapted to circumscribed space. Small trees are particularly convenient for pruning, for thinning, and gathering the fruit, for the comparative ease with which they can be suited with the soil most fit for them, whatever that of the garden they grow in may be, and the ease with which such trees can be shifted or removed at any time, or almost at any age.

This reduction of the luxuriance of the tree by curtailing the luxuriance of the root, may be effected by taking up the trees, pruning the roots, and putting them in again, or by cutting away a portion of the roots without further disturbing the tree. It is reckoned that trees of a rampant habit of growth may with advantage be reduced in root to the extent of one-sixth, those of medium habit one-fourth, and those of delicate habit a third.

The extremities of the roots, and roots inclined to shoot perpendicularly downwards, only should be pruned, and care must be taken not to injure the surface roots: these should, on the contrary, be encouraged to keep near the surface by the application of manure occasionally.

Our celebrated cultivator of fruit trees, Mr. Rivers, of Sawbridgeworth, is a great advocate of root-pruning, and recommends it for trees of cordon and pyramidal training, and for all dwarfs.

Some growers recommend lifting or removing trees every two years, if they grow in a very rich soil; but whatever may be said in favour of root-pruning by means of a trench, it is advisable so to adapt the soil and culture to trees as to avoid the need of positive removal.

For root-pruning by means of a trench, moist weather should be chosen soon after the gathering of the fruit, and a trench a foot and a half from the stem of the tree, if it be young, carefully opened, deep enough to bring the ends of the roots to sight. The horizontal roots should there be shortened with the pruning-knife, and wherever roots anywhere beneath the tree are taking a vertical growth, they should be cut through with a sharp spade; the trench is afterwards filled in with rotted dung and mould. The distance of the trench from the tree may vary with its age: say, if 18 inches for the first pruning, it may be 24 two years later, 30, 36, and so on.

If a tree is thriving with healthful but moderate growth, and maturing fine fruit in abundance in proportion to its size, and has space for its growth, let well alone; but if space be so great an object that the tree is outgrowing the room it has, and can have no more, or if it shows rampant growth and little fruit, try the effect of root-pruning.

CHAPTER VII.

PROTECTION.

ONE great drawback to the successful growth of fruit in England is the bitter weather of our late springs. There are few localities, except in the South-west, where fair promise in blossom is not frequently negatived by late, sharp, often sudden snaps of frost, unseasonable falls of snow, or hail-storms. Often our fruit trees have to bear up against the first and second in February and March, and the last in April and May, after a little genial promise of spring has encouraged the stone-fruit and pears into vegetation.

There are few fruit-growers who have not watched the opening buds with pleasure and hope, flattering themselves that the apparently settled spring weather, and daily increasing heat of the sun were making the expectation of fruit a reality, when a sudden night frost, not seeming much perhaps, or storm of snow or hail, has raised doubt and fear; they have watched the blossom after it, and soon the unmistakable black withering of the pistil tells the tale of mischief done, soon to be confirmed by the non-swelling of the fruit, and its final falling off.

This vexatious loss of fruit, sometimes year after year, renders some kind of protection to fruit trees almost necessary, in many localities, in the early spring. Apples often produce good crops, when pears and other fruits are cut off to a great extent, because they bloom later: our frosts and other inclemencies are seldom late enough to interfere with them, but the earlier blooming fruits almost as seldom entirely escape.

The best protection for wall fruit is a thin canvas, or other light material hung in front of the trees, touching the wall at the top and borne out from it at an angle to the bottom. Frost has such a downfalling tendency, that the most important thing is to give protection above the top of the tree. In fact frost so generally does mischief falling vertically, not piercing horizontally, that two or three feet breadth of covering fixed to the top of the wall, and carried out from it on a slant, will often save the crop.

In fixing the protecting material, great care must be taken that it cannot beat backwards and forwards upon the bloom, or chafe it in any way, or the mischief it may do may be greater than that from the weather.

Almost any material will do; it should be thin and light. Now that ladies' dresses are worn so full, the industrious may convert worn-out skirts into very good screens for fruit trees. A *very thin* material made of wool is perhaps the best of any, being a non-conductor of heat, and of a less clinging habit than cotton or linen. Bunting may often be bought cheap in the form of old flags, and it does very well.

Frigi domo is a material which has been much advertised for protecting trees from the late frosts, and from sun and wind when necessary. It is a mixture of hair and wool, a non-conductor of heat, thin and light. It may be bought at 1s. 9d. per yard, two yards wide; 2s. 8d. three yards wide; and 3s. 6d. four yards wide. A kind of thin canvas also is made on purpose for covering trees, which may be bought for 5d. per square yard, and the same length will last with care for seven years.

The protecting curtains, if I may so call them, should be fixed temporarily along the top of the wall, or hung on nails there, by means of little rings or loops along the upper edge. Poles fixed against the wall on a slant, with the bottom about three feet from the wall, will keep the curtain at a safe distance from the bloom.

Another apparatus for fixing the curtains is to fix poles on a slant, three feet from the wall at the bottom, and close against it at the top. Two feet from the bottom pegs are fixed in the poles, and stand out nine inches in front; the curtain is fixed on these pegs, and lies upon them, when it is not in use to cover the trees, and it is drawn up and let down by means of cords fixed to the top edge, and a ring and staple to the top of each pole.

A wide, overhanging coping to a wall offers much protection to the trees trained upon it.

Dwarf trees can easily be protected by means of a fixed framework round them, set in for the purpose. Fix four poles of exactly equal height, one at each corner of the tree, and a few inches taller than it, either with or without cross-bars, and fix over the top a square of grey calico, or any other cheap material. A piece of the same grey calico, or other material, may be tacked round the sides, leaving a vacancy at top and bottom for the free circulation of air.

Many other things may be used to protect dwarf trees. Flat branching little boughs, like pea sticks, or fir branches in a pretty close plantation, set half round the tree to windward, may save a crop.

As a preservative against still hoar-frost, when it seems severe enough to prove destructive, a little hay or withered fern may be spread over the top of the tree. These hoar-frosts are often sharp enough to do great mischief, therefore do not trust them in the case of any tree which is likely to bloom early, but before any blossom opens, set in brushwood sticks around, a few inches taller than it, and bending inward, so as to lean over it, and over their tops throw fern or hay, putting it so in amongst the end twigs that the wind will not carry it away.

A breadth of tiffany, or any other light fabric, may at night be thrown over the top of a dwarf tree, flowering a little before our late springs render it safe, and taken off in the morning, if sunshine succeeds frost.

A temporary tent-like house, made of any light fabric stretched over a light frame of wood, and fixed to the place where it is wanted for the time, by stakes, may be placed over early flowering trees, until the set fruit is safe. When a house of this kind is used, allowance should be made for the growth of the young trees it is meant to cover, as the owner will most likely not wish to have a new one every year, or even every two years. The roof is the important thing for keeping off frost, and the sides may be covered frames, to lift up or let down at pleasure, for which bits of strong leather, securely nailed, will make sufficiently good hinges. Houses like this might be made to take to pieces and fold together flat, for packing away when not in use, which would make them last a long time.

A simple, tolerably fine netting, especially if it be of wool, is often a sufficient protection to save the setting fruit.

With very small trees, sprays of gorse or fern may sometimes be tied, so as to shelter the early blossom; but in this and all protection, care must be taken that the screen used does not do harm by fretting the bloom or knocking against it.

The next consideration is *when* to give protection. Unless frost be so severe as to cut off the leaf-buds, the blossom-buds are pretty safe until they begin to swell out quite plump. From that time they want protection from frost, but they should not be deprived of any sunshine there may be. The time of the greatest danger to them is when the blossom is fully open, then if frost gets to it the pistil turns black, and the fruit is nowhere. When the fruit is formed and swells out plump, it is comparatively safe, but even long after that frost, snow, hail, and bitter winds may cut it off, and strew it in unsatisfactory showers around the tree. Begin, therefore, to protect before the blossom opens, and judgment, the locality and the weather, must decide when to take off the screens.

Our late frosts are our fruit's worst enemies; compared with the mischief they do, that worked by birds is small, and has, as compensation, great destruction of insects, more destructive by far than they. Carefully avoid injuring, as the garden's best friends, the wood-wren, the willow-wren or haybird, the golden-crested wren, the chiff-chaff, the nightingale, the whinchat, the stonechat, and the wheatear. Spare also the wagtails, the tree-pipet, or titlark, the meadow-pipet, the cuckoo, the fly-catcher, the flusher or lesser butcher-bird, and many others.

The common wren, the hedge-sparrow, the robin, the redstart, the tomtit, the coaltit, the marshtit, and the greater tit, eat some small fruit, and a little seed and grain, but pay for it all over and over again by the weeds and insects they destroy.

The blackcap, the babillard, the garden-warbler, the whitethroat, the missel-thrush, the song-thrush, and the blackbird, certainly do consume cherries and other fruit with little moderation, especially the thrushes and blackbirds, but they eat also so many insects, that it is better to scare them away at the time they can destroy most than to kill them.

Inventions for scaring birds must be constantly, entirely, and radically altered, as they soon get so accustomed to the sight of a scarecrow, and familiar with its appearance, that I have known a bird build in the habiliments of an old soldier set up to protect the garden. Noisy or moving scares are best, but they even must be often changed, or familiarity will breed contempt.

Dwarf trees and currant bushes may be netted, as an effectual protection from the depredations of the birds.

Wasps I believe cannot be warded off. The only thing to do with them is to carry the war into the enemy's country, by watching them home and destroying their nests.

Protection from the heat of the sun is seldom wanted in our climate, on the contrary, we should often be glad of more of it than we can get, and a sufficiently luxuriant growth of leaves will shelter enough.

Protection from wind in exposed localities is best managed by having dwarf trees, which may always be low, sheltered, and safe.

CHAPTER VIII.

DISEASES AND INSECTS.

ONE destructive disease of fruit trees, canker, has been described in the chapter on the choice of young trees. Canker, properly so called, is a kind of dry sore, but the name is also sometimes applied to a kind of ulcer discharging sap or gum.

Old trees are more frequently attacked by canker than young ones, and the golden pippin, about the oldest apple we have, suffers from it most injuriously. Irony gravel as a subsoil is sure to bring canker. Sour, badly-drained ground will also occasion it; several other inducing causes have been before mentioned, and it attacks the roots as well as the branches.

If it have greatly gained head it is incurable, and the only plan is to destroy the tree, improve the soil, if necessary, and plant a young tree in the place. A cankered tree is not worth grafting.

Sometimes the canker is on a limb which can be entirely removed: cut it out cleanly and entirely, and thin the tree so liberally generally as to leave no branches or even twigs to rub and chafe each other. If the tree be of a sluggish growth, it may be thoroughly cut back, but this will not do with trees of luxuriant growth, as their efforts to make more wood will increase the evil. In their case lessen the richness of the soil by mixing in less fertile earth, drift-sand, or something of that kind, avoid the use of manure in the neighbourhood of the tree, and cut away some of the roots. The golden pippin will bear plentiful pruning.

Unless trees are very old and far gone, canker may generally be got rid of by letting in plenty of air and light, by necessary improvement of the soil, by heading in, pruning, by cutting the tap-root, if it pierce downwards, and last, not least, by scrubbing the bark of trunk and branches as far as possible with soapsuds and urine, and covering up all wounds with cow manure beaten up with clay, to prevent the disease attacking them or spreading.

Old overgrown trees are often starved to death for want of manure, their owners neglecting to calculate how much large trees have to do with the nourishment they draw from an area of earth, small in proportion to their size. The quantity of manure to be given to fruit trees with advantage is a question which practice, experience, and reflection only can determine, and the circumstances of almost every tree may vary with regard to it. The thing to avoid in giving manure is the encouragement of a too rampant growth, at the expense of fruit. The thing to avoid in withholding it is starving the tree, by want of nourishment, into premature decay, and the production of poor, immature fruit, cracking instead of ripening. Moderately mulching large old trees, which are plentiful bearers, can seldom do harm, and once in three years a little of the surface-mould round them may be taken up in

October, slush from the manure reserve laid on, and covered again with the earth. A good pruning should accompany this treatment, and it will often renew the constitution of the tree, and restore the fruit in size and clearness of skin.

Mildew is a troublesome and injurious fungous growth, especially attacking peaches, nectarines, apricots, and vines. It is said to be generated in the earth, the result of too much moisture at the roots, and thence to communicate itself generally over the tree, or over a portion of it, by means of myriads of minute seeds which are wafted through the air. It is worst in damp, muggy seasons, and I think draught developes it. It acts upon the tree by spreading over it, filling up the pores, and impeding respiration. There are several kinds which infest the rose tree. That which attacks stone fruit is the *Oidium erysephoides*, and that of the vine, *Oidium Tuckeri*, which will cover the fruit so as to render it useless.

It may be discouraged at the root of the tree by draining and by digging in lime, and the tree itself should have a due mixture of warmth and moisture; but sulphur is the popular and invariably used remedy. With vines especially the sulphur is often used excessively, by dusting it over leaves and fruit; machines are made, at a cost of two or three shillings each, for diffusing it equally; but the remedy of covering grapes with sulphur is so nearly as bad as the disease, that it is best to use all possible caution for keeping it off, by protecting the roots from stagnant damp, by constantly regulating the temperature of the house, by guarding against draught, a cold damp, or a hot dry heat.

Some administer the sulphur in fumes by mixing it with whitewash, and washing the hot-water pipes, or, if flues are used, by washing with it the sides farthest from the stove; or sulphur may be placed on a hot-water plate and the water kept boiling below with a lamp. A kind of paint for washing over the stems and branches may be made by mixing 1 lb. of soft soap and 1 lb. of sulphur into a paste with warm water, and a small wine-glass of spirit of turpentine. Another recipe is to boil half a pound of tobacco for an hour in a covered saucepan, mix the decoction with the soap, &c., and add water enough to make two gallons of the whole.

Another mixture for the stems may be made by beating together half a pound of sulphur, a quarter of a pound of soft soap, and two ounces of pepper, stir it into two gallons of water, let it boil for twenty minutes, thicken it with lime until it is thick enough to lay on in a coat, like paint with a brush, and stir in soot enough to make it a pale slate-colour, that it may be less of an eyesore upon the trees than glaring white would be.

A good wash may be made of clay, sulphur, and water, which will very likely clog less than these.

Except in extreme cases, it is better to avoid washes of the thick consistence of paint, as they cannot but be injurious by excluding air and impeding respiration.

Exudation of gum sometimes injures trees which are subject to it, especially the cherry. Avoid planting in over-rich soil and other circumstances likely to create too luxuriant a growth, and take care that the tree does not get wounded or rubbed in the bark; both causes occasion escape of gum. Bleeding, or the loss of sap by a wound, is only the same thing in another kind of tree. Vines will bleed enough to weaken or injure them greatly if they are injudiciously cut at a wrong season.

When trees die, apparently without rhyme or reason, it is generally because they have sent their roots down to an ungenial subsoil. Preventive measures are to shift the tree, if it be not too old, to make a trench round it and cut the roots which are running down too deep, and by encouraging the roots to keep near the surface of the ground by a little gentle forking and mulching.

The insects which injure fruit trees and destroy the fruit, are almost too numerous to name—their name is legion. Those which attack the trunk of the tree are perhaps the most destructive and the most powerful.

The stag-beetle clings to the trunks of trees and lays its eggs, and the larva works its way into the wood and commits depredations in that form for three years.

The goat-moth is yet more destructive in its caterpillar form, eating into the wood of fruit trees for two or three years before its change. It is the *Cossus ligniperda* of naturalists; the caterpillar, which is also called the auger-worm, is about four inches in length, dark red on the back, and flesh-coloured underneath, with a black head, smooth, shining skin, and a few short hairs about the body. Before taking the chrysalis shape it changes to yellow. The chrysalis is yellow with pointed spines, and it is generally deposited just inside the opening in the tree. In June or July the moth, which measures nearly three inches across the wings, and is of a sober hue, little distinguishable from the trunk, emerges from its hole. The female is said to lay 1,000 eggs in the bark of the tree, and the little caterpillars live at first in the bark, and afterwards take to their work of destruction of boring into the wood. When the worm is detected, by its excrement, great mischief is already done, but it should be picked out if possible, or killed by thrusting a wire up the hole. Its name of goat-moth is derived from the strong smell of both the moth and worm.

A plump beetle, resembling the rose-beetle, *Gnorimus nobilis*, also eats into wood, and remains in the destructive stage three years; and the caterpillar of the Wood Leopard Moth, a black and white moth, also injures the wood.

Against these injurious insects many birds—especially fly-catchers and the tits—wage incessant war, running up and carefully overlooking every inch of bark and picking out the larvæ.

The American or cotton blight has been mentioned in the chapter on choosing fruit trees. It is the *Eriosoma mali* of some entomologists, and is named by others *E. lanigera*, or *Aphis lanigera*. It is very destructive to apple trees, and spreads and increases with amazing quickness: it also sometimes attacks other fruit trees. It is called the cotton blight from a white cottony secretion in which it envelopes itself, and from which it may be easily detected and destroyed. The insect itself is roundish, shiny, and dark brown in colour, giving out a red dye when crushed. They attack the tree underground as well as above, and crowd about the trunk and branches. Scrape and scrub the branches thoroughly clean with soft soap and water, or ammoniacal liquor, bare the roots and use ammoniacal liquor to them also. Turpentine destroys them, but it must be sparingly applied, as it injures foliage it happens to touch.

The apple-bark beetle, *Bostrichus dispar*, is very injurious to the apple on the Continent, but is not very common in England. The female bores into the bark of the tree to deposit her eggs, with numerous and extensive perforations. The alburnum is the seat of its depredations.

Insects which live upon and destroy the leaves are about as destructive as those that eat into the wood, since they are more numerous, and destroy the vital energy of the tree by rendering the leaves which carry on its living functions useless for that purpose.

The whole extensive family of scale insects, *Coccus*, rob the leaves and stems of their juices, and will kill what they attack, if they are left undisturbed. They stick close to leaves and stems like oblong scales; the females are stationary, but the male insect has wings, and is almost too minute to see with the unaided eye. I believe there is no remedy but hand-picking, washing, and scrubbing. In greenhouses they are most troublesome pests. Turpentine brushed over the plant, or conveyed to it in fumes, destroys them; but whatever plan is followed, the all-important thing is to attack them directly they appear, before they get ahead at all.

Coccus adonidum, or the mealy-bug, is soft-bodied, in shape a little like a wood-louse, covered with a white appearance, like meal, and giving out a crimson dye when crushed. Some persons get rid of them when they abound by the use of the washes given above for mildew. It attacks vines, pine apples, and any plants it can get at, being very destructive to myrtles, fuchsias, and such like. *Coccus vitis*, or the vine-scale, attacks vines indoors and out of doors, peaches, nectarines, and plums. They are oblong and convex in form, sticking so close down to the stem as to be detected only by looking close at the plant, light-coloured while young, and brown as they get old and firm. *Coccus hesperidum*, which is such an enemy to the orange tree, is similar. They fix themselves on the under sides of the leaves and also along the stems. *Coccus Bromeliæ*, or pine-apple scale, infests that fruit.

A kind of scale insect which infests the pear, *Aspidiotus ostræformis*, is similar to the scale insect, and to be dislodged by the same treatment.

Aphides are almost universal in their depredations, so few are the plants and trees they let alone. We all know how destructive they are among our roses, and in fact among all our choice, tender, succulent plants. As they take their colour very much from the food they feed on, it seems likely that there are really fewer varieties than naturalists name. *Aphis pyrimali* attack our apples and pears. *A. Persicæ* devotes itself to the peach and nectarine. *A. pruni* infests plum trees, and is of a very pale green. *A. cerasi* is black: in damp soils it attacks the morello cherry, overrunning the under sides of the leaves. *A. corily*, the nut aphis, is of a pale green. *A. ribis*, the currant aphis, and *A. ribis nigra*, the black currant aphis, attack currants; curiously enough, the first is darker than the last.

To get rid of aphides, syringing with a decoction of elder-tops, tobacco-water, or soapsuds, on two or three following days, is good. Fumigating with tobacco smoke, where it can be managed, is also good.

The aphis appears very early on the peach. When wall fruit trees are infested, they should be taken down from the wall in the early spring and well scrubbed. If shreds are used, provide new ones. Giving plants and trees plenty of air and light, is the best preventive against this, the scale insect, and thrips; as, on the contrary, want of air, and too much heat, are sure to bring them.

Thrips ochraceus is most disagreeable in its attacks on ripe plums, peaches, and nectarines, soiling and spoiling the fruit and making it fall. It is of an ochreous colour, and the body is hairy. A good remedy is Scotch snuff, spread by means of the machine used for dusting sulphur over vines.

The mite family, *Acari*, are destructive in proportion to numerical force, and difficult to deal with from their extreme minuteness. *A. tellarius*, the red spider, is the worst of the lot, almost covering the under surfaces of the leaves, impeding respiration by spreading a minute web wherever they go, and sucking the juices until the foliage loses colour, becomes dry, and is useless for its office of carrying on necessary circulation. The insect is so small that it can scarcely be detected by the unassisted eye, and it is one of the gardener's greatest pests. In form it rather resembles a spider; sometimes it is yellowish, sometimes brown, and sometimes of a dull red, and it has a dark spot on each side of the back. It is especially destructive in greenhouses and hothouses, which have been kept too hot and dry, but it also attacks (out of doors) beans, lime trees, apple, pear, and plum trees, and destroys cucumbers. Make a paint by beating up a quarter of a pound of soft soap in a gallon of warm water, mix in clay enough to make it like paint, and a little soot to deaden the colour. Stir in four good handfuls of sulphur, and keep it stirred up while you paint with it the stems of fruit trees that are infested, and the walls behind such as are planted against walls. The beginning of April is the time to use it. The lime-wash used in greenhouses should have a good proportion of sulphur mixed with it. Syringing with water is good, as is also fumigating with sulphur or turpentine; but care must be taken that the sulphur does not take fire, which would destroy the plants: it begins to vapourize at $170°$, to which it may be raised, on plates over boiling water, or on hot-water pipes. Syringe afterwards.

A. geniculatus is a glossy, brownish-red mite, which collects on the bark of plum and other trees. It may be effectually dislodged by a touch of turpentine, or by the use of gas ammoniacal liquor. *A. holosericeus*, another Acarus, is distinguished by its scarlet colour, and others infest various plants in our gardens.

The *Psylla*, or Chermes, is something like a large aphis. *P. pyri* is often to be found on pear trees, and occasionally on the apple. It appears in May, like a crimson aphis, shaded with black. The eggs, resembling the pollen of a flower, are laid in great numbers on the young leaves, flowers, and newly formed fruit. As the insects grow, they become darker, reddish on the breast, something like bugs in appearance, and travel downwards to the bearing wood and shoots of the year before, where they fix themselves in rows. Before the last change they fix themselves singly to leaves, and change to the winged insect, which is of a beautiful green, with red eyes and perfectly white wings. After a few days, the colour partly changes to orange, and the fly takes to the wing. The apple thermes, *P. mali*, appears later. The eggs are first white, afterwards yellow, rather pointed at both ends, and often arranged in an exact pattern. It destroys the buds, and is different in appearance from the pear thermes, but the winged insect is equally beautiful. For all (one attacks the fig) on fruit trees, camelias, or roses, syringe with tobacco-water first, and afterwards with pure water.

The saw-fly, *Selandria Ethiops*, or the shiny grub, so called on account of a dark slimy matter which covers the body, chiefly attacks pear trees, but is sometimes found on the cherry. The grub is about half an inch long, dark, from the slimy black-green fluid enveloping it, and larger near the head than at the other end. In October it changes to a brown cocoon, and in June or July becomes the winged insect, a shiny black fly, with yellowish tips to the legs, about the third of an inch across the extended wings. The eggs are deposited on the upper surface of the leaves.

Caterpillars are many of them most destructive to our fruit trees, occasionally making a clean sweep of all the leaves on a tree. The magpie moth, a yellowish-white flat moth, with a little orange, measuring about an inch and a half across the wings, and irregularly covered with black spots, produces the gooseberry caterpillar, *Abraxas grossulariata*, which sometimes leaves our gooseberry and currant trees without a leaf. The little looping caterpillar is yellowish-white, with an orange stripe down each side, and numerous black spots about it. The butterflies are plentiful in July and August. The female lays her eggs on a leaf, and in September the caterpillars are said to hatch out, ready to begin their depredations in the spring. They begin upon gooseberries and red currants, but after they have finished them they will feed on sloes, peaches, and almonds. The chrysalis is black, with orange rings round the pointed end. Hand-picking is the best cure. Dusting with the powder of white helebore is also very good.

The caterpillar of *Tinea qadella*, or small ermine moth, appears in autumn, from eggs laid near the bloom-buds of the apple, pear, Euonymus and hawthorn, in June and July; they enclose the twigs with a web, and the following spring they attack the petals of the flower and the calyx. The caterpillar is a dull dark colour, with a black head, and the moth is white with black dots on the wings, minute and pretty. The pear-blister moth, *Tinea clerckella*, is active, minute, glossy, and the wings are orange, spotted. In August the caterpillars raise dark brown blisters on the leaves of pear trees, and occasionally attack the apple also. If the tree is small, and the mischief taken in time, the injured leaves can be picked off and burnt. Washing with soapsuds at the end of May, when the moths are laying their eggs, is recommended. The triple-spotted currant tinea, *Tinea capitella*, in its larva stage eats into the pith of the young shoots of the currant in spring and the larva of *Tinea corticella* spoils apple trees by establishing itself under the bark.

The worm belonging to the apricot moth, *Pædisca Angustiorana*, is a small yellowish-green, wriggling little caterpillar that rolls itself up in the leaf of peach, nectarine, and apricot, and is very active at making its escape by dropping down by a thread. Throughout May watch for rolled up leaves and destroy them as they appear. It changes into a brown, shining chrysalis, rolled in leaves, which should also be sought for and destroyed. The moth is a tiny brown thing, which deposits its eggs upon the branches.

The ripening fruit upon our trees has as inveterate enemies as the trees themselves.

Earwigs, *Forficulæ auricularis*, eat into peaches, plums, and other luscious fruits in the night, and in the day hide away in dark recesses. The way to trap them is to reverse crab or lobster claws, small pots, or conical screws of paper, on the tops of sticks set in the ground near the places they frequent. The earwigs crawl into the dark recesses of the traps, and should be shaken out and killed every morning. They have wings, and use them at times, so that anything to destroy them placed round the stem of the tree is of very little use.

Slugs and snails destroy choice fruit by eating it, and by crawling over it, leaving their slime, which by its glossy trail gives evidence where they have been. Handpicking is good in the case of both, especially of snails, which can be hunted for and found in cracks in the walls, behind stones, and in such like out-of-the-way corners. Both snails and slugs are night-feeders, retiring and hiding by day.

Lime and salt destroy slugs. In the evening water the earth round the tree with lime-water, then strew lime over the ground, and at the end of a week give a surface-dressing of salt, allowing a bushel to a rood of land. Wall fruit trees infested with slugs may be syringed with lime-water. Cabbage leaves dipped in greasy water, or little piles of brewer's grains, will attract them, when they may be caught and killed. Continual stirring of the earth does good; and they may be kept off wall fruit by strewing lime along the top and along the bottom of the wall, and renewing it once a week.

The figure-of-eight moth, *Episema cœrula-cephala*, in its caterpillar form destroys the bloom of apples, pears, and cherries, besides eating the leaves of these and of peaches. The moth has bluish-grey upper wings, with a spot on each something like a figure of 8. It is very destructive, and should be destroyed whenever it is possible.

The codlin moth, *Carpocapsa pomonella*, is most destructive to apples, the female depositing her eggs singly, one in the eye of each young apple, pushing the ovipositor between the divisions of the calyx. Here the egg hatches, the little grub eats its way into the fruit, feeds first on the pulp, at last on the pips, the apple falls, the grub creeps out—in the night it is supposed—and crawls up the trunk of the tree, where, hidden away in a crack of the bark, it makes a smooth kind of nest and a little white silk case, and changes to the chrysalis. When apples are picked up (the ground is covered wherever these depredators exist), the hole must be looked for, and if it is opened the insect has escaped, most likely effectually, for when the apple is down, the grub soon makes good its retreat: all worm-eaten fruit that can be detected should be made safe earlier.

The moth is, with closed wings, less than half an inch long, in shades of brown beautifully variegated. The grub is of a dirty-white colour, with a brown head, having six feet in front and two behind. The codlin is more subject to it than other apples, and it is difficult to get rid of it, but much may be done by collecting the apples, *as they fall*, and destroying the grubs, and by searching for and destroying the chrysalises in the crevices of the bark. Some naturalists call it *Carpocapsa pomonella*, the name above given, others *Tinea pomonella*, *Pyralis pomona*, or *Tortrix pomoniana*.

The *Curculio*, a large family of weevils, are many of them most destructive to fruit trees. *C. pyri* resembles the apple weevil. The stem-boring weevil, *C. alliariæ*, is iridescent black, and bores the shoots and grafts of young fruit trees in June and July. *C. Bacchus* lays its eggs in the fruit of the apple in June and July. *C. betuleti*, the vine weevil, is a bright blue-black: it rolls up the leaf of the vine as a nest for its eggs, and also attacks the pear in June and July. *C. cupreus*, the copper-coloured weevil, attacks the leaves and young shoots of plums and apricots in June and July. *C. nucum*, the nut weevil, demolishes our nuts: the best thing is to shake the bushes and collect and destroy the worm-eaten nuts that fall. *C. oblongus* is oblong, of a reddish-brown, and feeds on the young leaves of peaches, apricots, plums, pears, and apples in May. *C. tenebricosus* is a great enemy to the apricot. The crevices in old walls often harbour them, and had better be filled up with mortar or cement, and if the larvæ are about the foot of the wall, a top-dressing of soot will do good. Infusion of tobacco or quassia does good.

Curculio pomorum, or *Anthonymus pomorum*, the apple weevil, is, perhaps, the worst of all this destructive family. The mature insect is a little beetle about a quarter of an inch long, which hides itself in the bark of apple trees in winter. In the spring the female lays her eggs, one in each flower-bud; these hatch into little white grubs, which destroy the flowers, and soon change into the beetles or weevils which feed on the leaves in summer, and are not often seen.

The weevils should be sought for in their beetle form in winter, when they may be found hidden in the bark of trees or under stones.

The winter moth, *Cheimatobia brumata*, is most destructive to the apple blossom, as well as to the leaves of many trees, and from living well through the winter, it is abundant and difficult to deal with.

The lackey moth, *Clisiocampa neustria*, lays a great number of eggs in wide compact bands round the small branches of pear and other trees: the caterpillars, when they hatch, collect in large nests at the forks of small branches, where they may be sought for and destroyed, taking care that none drop by a thread and so escape. The *Tortrix* is a kind of moth with many varieties, very injurious to fruit.

As valuable and industrious destroyers of mischievous insects, take care that no harm happens to either ladybirds, toads, or frogs.

CHAPTER IX.

TOOLS AND STORING-ROOMS.

The chief tools required exclusively in the fruit garden are good saws, well set; one widely set, for cutting moist green wood, and good keen pruning-knives. In all things of this kind it is the most convenient, as well as the best economy, to buy things of first-rate quality, and to take good care of them. All steel articles should have frequent and plentiful oiling with pure neat's-foot oil. They should also be kept in a dry place, and never left out in the wet or damp.

Pruning-scissors are of all shapes and sizes, set at all kinds of angles, but those for fruit trees are generally set straight, on either long or short handles.

A good pair of rose-scissors is necessary for cutting twigs and all young shoots, and a pair of long-handled cutting shears, capable of severing any branch up to the size of a man's wrist, kept sharp and in good order, is also necessary. All cutting and pruning for which one or other of these is not adapted, may very well fall to the lot of the pruning-knife or the saw.

Spades, rakes, hoes, forks, picks, and all the other tools belonging to the ordinary kitchen garden, may of course come into use from time to time, among the fruit trees, too, but use them there with caution. It is not wise ever to dig among the roots of fruit trees, or to plant crops so near to them that they can, by possibility, interfere with them. A little gentle, careful forking is all in the shape of digging that should approach the roots of trees, as the object in working the soil about them is to encourage the roots to spread near the surface of the ground, not on any account to induce them to strike downwards, nor to injure the tender rootlets.

A wheelbarrow for conveying earth, manure, or other things, ladders and steps of different heights for reaching tall trees, either to cut them or to gather the fruit, and baskets, are indispensable. A budding-knife is convenient for its own work; and there are many natty contrivances which may be had or done without at pleasure.

Averruncators are small, powerful shears on long handles, for pruning high trees; the price is about 20s. each. There are also appropriate scissors sold for thinning grapes, and various other purposes. Hammers and a few tools of that kind are occasionally wanted. In the neighbourhood of London, trees are trained by means of shreds and cast-iron wall nails. In some parts of the country nails for fixing the trees to are fixtures on the wall, and the trees are attached to them by withies (willow twigs). In other parts, again, tarred shreds of cord are used.

A good fruit-room is a necessary adjunct to every garden wherein fruit prospers, for most fruit has to be gathered before it is ripe, to prevent its being spoiled by falling, which it will do as soon as it is perfectly ripe. When the fruit has attained its full size, and will leave the tree easily by simply lifting, not breaking, the stalk, the ripening process, a formation of sugar and attendant exhalation of carbonic acid and water, goes on as well when it is stored as on the tree, for by that time the functions of the leaves, being no longer necessary, cease.

The apple and pear room should be neither hot nor cold, uniform in temperature, and dry. Some persons recommend a situation below the ground, that the temperature may not fluctuate; but it is important that it should be airy and dry, and therefore I think a good room above ground better. Let it have easily regulated, good ventilation, and a north aspect, with means for effectually keeping out frost. An underground storing place, to be sufficiently dry, should be drained, floored with concrete, and the foundation of the walls laid in cement. This will not only keep the place dry, but it will effectually keep out rats and mice—great pests among the fruit. The best temperature for a fruit-room is never above 60°

nor below 40°; the nearer the thermometer can be kept to this the better.

If a fruit-room have to be built, and expense be no object, there is great advantage in making it with double walls, leaving a space between the two, which keeps out alike the cold of winter and the heat of summer. There should be a cavity of about three inches; and there is no better non-conductor of heat than these hollow walls. If the fruit-room be a simple, small building, constructed for the purpose thus with double walls, the same pains must be taken with the roof, as regards the non-conducting of heat; it should be double, or there should be a ceiling, and the space above well and closely packed with trusses of straw. Generally, however, a room in the house, among the offices, or forming a portion of some range of buildings on the premises, will do better, and be more under control than a detached building made on purpose.

For ventilation there is nothing better than a good full-sized window or windows, according to the size of the room, to reach up to the ceiling, and to open at the top and at the bottom. When abundance of fruit is housed in the autumn, air must be let in and damp let out; air let in near the top of the room will create a brisk circulation, and the egress of a volume of air, by opening the window wide, is sometimes necessary to dispel damp. Fruit keeps best if kept pretty nearly in the dark, so that there should be dark blinds wherewith to darken the room, but means of admitting light, without cold, to examine, pick out, and arrange the fruit. In severe frost the windows must be matted up to keep it out.

A fruit-room may generally be kept to a temperature which will preserve fruit for family use throughout the winter.

A framework like a bottle rack, with the tiers very close together, is good for apples, and, with some reservation, for pears too. The cross shelves on which to lay out the fruit may be of the common double laths, which are bought by the bundle; and they need not of necessity be fixed, but may be ranged on the frame, nearer or farther apart, according to the size of the fruit to lie on them, at the time it is laid out. Frames like this may partly surround the room: the depth from back to front may be from $1\frac{1}{2}$ to 2 feet, that the back may be reached without difficulty, and the tiers 6 or 9 inches apart, to admit the hand above the fruit. These frames should be looked over pretty often, and the bad or specked fruit picked out. All kinds should be allowed to get dry before they are stored.

Apples of all varieties keep capitally in a fruit-room. They should be arranged each kind by itself, and the earliest the most come-at-able. Many kinds of pears keep well in the same way; or they may, when they are dry, be arranged in new or thoroughly clean garden pots, or unglazed pans, covered each with a pan or piece of slate, and stored where frost cannot get to them. Of course the fruit will ripen the sooner if the room be warm, and some for earliest use may be hastened by laying them out in the sun.

Mr. Rivers, than whom we can scarcely have a better judge, recommends keeping pears for the winter in a greenhouse, but I have tried it without a good result. "My pears," he writes, "have been laid out on the front bench of a lean-to greenhouse, the stage at the back being occupied by camelias. The glass over the pears was shaded until the end of November, the house ventilated, and the camelias watered as if the pears were not there. In severe frost the temperature was kept just above freezing. The autumn pears ripened slowly, and were excellent in flavour, the late pears kept until April, but then shrivelled; as the sun gained power the house became too hot and dry. I should therefore recommend winter pears to be stored in covered pots or jars early in December, and kept in the greenhouse."

Choice pears may be wrapped each one in paper, and ranged one layer deep in shallow boxes or drawers. Thus packed, one box at a time can be removed into a warmer room, to ripen thoroughly.

Quinces and medlars will keep quite as well as apples

with no more care. Nuts should be kept in a rather damper place.

The good keeping of fruit greatly depends on the care with which it is gathered, as the slightest bruise will spoil the keeping. Many amateur fruit-growers gather their own fruit, and unless the gardener be unusually careful and dexterous, there is scarcely a job in the whole garden on which a gentleman can better bestow his own personal work and attention.

The fruit should, one by one, be quietly removed from the tree and gently laid, not thrown, into the basket. Apples and pears should never, on any account, be poured from one basket to another, or on to the floor, but gently removed, if necessary, by hand. It is advisable not only to pick the fruit with the greatest care and gentleness, but to avoid shifting it from basket to basket. Lay it softly in the first basket, in that convey it to where it is to be spread out to dry, and with equal care lay out all that are sound and good, and pick out for immediate use (for self or friends or pig, according to degree of damage) all that are touched by an insect, even in a slight degree, and all that have a suspicion of a bruise. The way often followed of *throwing* the apples or other fruit into a basket as they are gathered, and pouring them from one basket to another, or upon the ground, cannot fail to lead to plenty of decayed fruit and proportionate disappointment.

Fruit-rooms are sometimes warmed artificially with flues, or a stove not in the room itself, but in an adjoining cupboard; but a little management will, almost for certain, keep out frost and preserve fruit through our winters.

Choice fruit for the London markets is packed in small boxes or baskets, each fruit separately wrapped in paper or wool, according to what it is, and the interstices filled up with bits of paper rolled up, or something similarly yielding, yet firm enough to keep the fruit from shifting. I have known apples and pears keep very well in a large press or cupboard, but a room better supplied with air is preferable. Apples may also be stored in hampers, with straw ranged between the layers, and kept in a cellar, but this precludes, or renders very troublesome, the necessary overlooking which economy demands.

CHAPTER X.

THE PEAR TREE AND ITS PRODUCE.

PERHAPS there is no fruit more popular in England than the pear, *Pyrus communis*, and no country in which it is finer than it is in ours; for although many of our splendid sorts are from France and Belgium, where scientific culture brings them to great size and perfection, none are so fine *in flavour* as those ripened, under favourable circumstances, by our milder sun. Even the pear-famed Channel Islands must yield the palm to England in that one point of flavour in the pears.

The best soil for pear trees is a sound loam, rather clayey than sandy. In Jersey, where pears do so well, light, sandy soil is very general, but it is where the heavier soil prevails that the pears do really well, and prosper year after year. Light, poor land, and cold, wet clay are equally bad, and a dry subsoil is necessary for success. Pears thrive pretty well in any ordinary soil, so it be in good heart; and manuring is not necessary with such, and must always be bestowed with great caution. In orchards for the cultivation of trees of large size, the soil should be quite two feet deep, but for trees of a more dwarfed habit a foot and a half is sufficient. In sandy loam, or any soil which is too dry for them, the fruit is apt to crack.

Grafting and budding are the usual modes of propagation. The free stock, or wild seedling, is calculated for growing large trees for orchards, and the quince stock is best for garden culture, it being of a moderate, compact habit of growth. The advantage of compactly grown trees, whether as bushes, pyramids, espaliers, or any other kind of training, is so very great, as regards easy culture, safety to the fruit, and beauty, that it seems almost a pity tall trees should be planted in gardens, to grow beyond all management, give great trouble in pruning, gathering, &c., and then to have half the fruit sacrificed by being blown down from its dangerous elevation. The great thing in favour of large trees is the abundant crops they will produce, if they are kept well thinned out; but the small trees, scientifically pruned, will produce abundant crops too, in proportion to the ground occupied *and shaded*, and of a much finer quality. Better have one basket of really superior pears, than two or three which are only second-rate. Budding is sometimes, but not often, practised.

Young trees are raised from seed in a kind of wholesale way, by burying the decaying fruit, until February, then mixing them up with a quantity of sand to separate the seed and pulp. All is then sown, and the young seedlings are left to themselves for a length of time. To raise seedlings with more care, the plumpest seeds—those which are plump on both sides, not flat on one side, one from each of the finest pears on the finest trees, fine flavoured and genially ripened—should be chosen, and sown not more than six in each pot. Label them and put them aside in a safe place, to come up in the spring, giving just a little water now and then. Some recommend keeping the seed until February, and sowing it then. It must be kept safe from mice, which are very fond of it, especially when it is germinating.

In June the young plants may be potted singly for another year, for the sake of safety while so small, or planted out in a safe border. Those which seem most promising may be hastened to show their quality by grafting from the young tree on a bearing old tree, or on a quince stock, when it is reckoned they bear in about half the time they would take if left to themselves.

In spring, the bearing pear trees want little but watching, which the amateur pear-grower, if he be fond of his trees, is pretty sure to give them in liberal supply.

They should be now, as left by good pruning of the year before, compact, shorn of all redundant and mischievous growth, and well supplied with fruit-spurs. No cutting back must be resorted to until the fruit is set and swelling. At this stage all that the watchful cultivator can do is to ward off destruction from the blossom and the tender fruit, by giving safe protection, if possible, from frost and storms, and hunting and destroying weevils and chrysalises hidden away in the bark or elsewhere. The earliest process to be resorted to in the way of pruning, is to rub off the buds which are likely to produce superabundant and crowded shoots. With wall trees, all buds that are likely to produce shoots growing outwards are to be rubbed off. This may be done in May. As soon as the buds swell, the leaf-buds and the flower-buds may be distinguished, not only by their situation, but from the leaf-buds being longer made and less plump than the bloom-buds. In June, begin pinching back all the little side-shoots. When they have made six or eight leaves, pinch them back to four leaves, and if the spurs put out young shoots again, pinch them back to one leaf only, always remembering to leave the leading side and top shoots to grow and draw up the sap until the end of summer, as recommended in the chapter on pruning. Continue this pinching back of small shoots throughout the summer, and cut back the leading shoots, until now left growing, about the end of August.

Pear trees intended to grow up into tall standards should have a straight, healthy stem, dividing at the top into four well-placed shoots of about equal strength, to form afterwards the leading branches; and the stem should be kept upright with a good firm stake, that it may grow into a straight trunk. In after years, as the head grows large, the branches must be thinned out, so that no one can interfere with another.

For wall or espalier training, little trees should have one stem, with side branches on two sides, and the front and back shoots should be cleanly pruned away. One shoot on each side will do; two on each side are better, and, for the sake of beauty and uniformity, they should agree one side with the other. The buds which tend backwards, or which are likely to grow out in front, should be rubbed off, unless much needed where they grow, in which case the shoots may be trained in.

The spurs on a pear tree should be short and far apart. Long spurs, crowded together, will never produce fine fruit. Where they are too crowded cut out, and where they are too long shorten them; but there will be little occasion for this with trees under careful culture.

There is another summer work for the pear-grower: besides pruning back the young shoots, he must thin out the pears with a continually watchful eye. Nature does the first pear-thinning, when the young pears which fail to shape and swell shrivel and drop off by hundreds. These, when they fall off, generally, unless frost or hail have done a sweeping work of destruction, leave quite as many plump, swelling little nobs of pears as is good for the tree, and plenty of work in thinning besides.

Avoid beginning to thin the pears too early; rather wait to see what the spring rains and stormy weather may accomplish in that way; but when the pears swell so as to approach, or in the slightest degree threaten to crowd each other, thin out liberally. The late pears may have more liberal thinning out than those which ripen in the autumn, because the last have to endure the winds and storms of autumn at a time when approaching maturity makes them less firm upon the tree, so that they will to a great extent thin themselves, and that, if it comes after a very plentiful, artificial thinning, may leave the trees quite too thin of fruit for the time of gathering. In July or August, according to the forwardness of the season, thin Chaumontels to the extent of leaving no more than two to each bunch; Louise Bonne, and other comparatively early kinds, need not be thinned nearly so much. In thinning, as in all other operations connected with fruit culture, experience and watchful care and observation must guide the hand. The eye must aid the hand, for every pear that is taken away before the worm makes its escape, will save great loss in years to come.

The way of gathering pears and other fruit has been already spoken of. The time of gathering varies with each particular sort, and varies also to some extent in different localities. In warm, sheltered spots, fruit ripens early; and the difference between the West Country or the Channel Islands, and the middle of England, or even the neighbourhood of London, is as much as a month; and the north of Scotland ripens fruit with even a greater difference still.

When the pears begin to fall, though it may be but in small numbers, we must watch for the right time to gather them. The rule to follow is to gather them when by just raising the pear it will leave the tree readily, without any effort to break the stalk: if any pull is required, the time for gathering has not arrived, and the fruit so gathered would shrivel instead of ripen. The time for gathering the few kinds particularized as fit for moderate gardens is given, but it may vary with localities and seasons; the rule of taking the pears when they will readily leave the tree may always apply.

When the pears are gathered, they must be so well stored that the earlier sorts will keep good and fit for use throughout their season, and the late kinds keep up a good supply throughout the winter and spring months. A cool, dry room, such a fruit-room as was described in the last chapter, is good for preserving the main stock from decay. Several of our finest kinds, however, require more warmth to finish the ripening, and give them the full, luscious, delicious flavour they should have. The coolish room is necessary to keep the supply continuous for a length of time, and more warmth is wanted at last to finish the ripening. Just to finish off the pears, about a week, say, before they are wanted, bring them into a temperature of 55° to 60°: they may be laid in a greenhouse with that temperature, or kept until used in the dining or common sitting-room.

CHAPTER XI.

THE SUMMER AND AUTUMN PEAR SUPPLY.

In the choice of kinds, most private growers are anxious to keep up a supply for family use throughout the season, having one or more summer sorts, according to the ground at command; a few first-class varieties of autumn-ripening pears, generally so much finer in flavour; and some to come in from the middle of winter to the end of spring, often better in all points than any, provided really good and productive trees can be obtained.

The Jargonelle is perhaps the best early pear for a garden which is small, or of only moderate dimensions, as it is a plentiful bearer, will keep better than most early pears, and is of a good size, juicy, melting, and finer in flavour than any equally early. It will flourish in almost any garden, and on a wall it will produce as far north as pears will grow. It is said to do best on the pear stock, and to be gritty at the core if grown on the quince, and it makes fine, large, well-grown trees, but Mr. Rivers recommends it for bush culture also.

One fine, productive Jargonelle pear tree gives no bad supply for a family, and there is less objection to its growing tall than in the case of kinds which have to bear autumn wind-storms, for it ripens by the middle of August, and is done with by about the end. It is the *Grosse cuisse Madame* of French growers. The fruit is greenish-yellow, with sometimes a tinge of brownish-red on the sunny side, rather pyramidal, long and large, with an open eye, long segments of calyx, and a longish stalk, obliquely inserted. If some are gathered before they are ripe, and stored in a cool fruit-room, they will ripen more gradually and keep longer than those left to ripen on the tree.

The Windsor is a very old sort, and popular from being early, a pretty good, often an abundant bearer, juicy and sweet. The tree is not hardy, being liable to canker if it be grown on a gravelly or cold, clayey soil. Some trees have the habit of bearing a great lot of poor, small fruit, such as we see in quantities sold cheap enough in the streets of London in summer. It is a pretty-looking pear, being yellow, with bright red on one side, and it ripens the end of August. In size it varies very much, but sometimes it is very good in that point. The eye is small, prominently placed, the stalk short, the flesh white, and the juice sweet, with a little astringent flavour.

William's Bouchrétien is large and handsome, similar to the Windsor in taste, but with a musky flavour. It is ripe about the same time, and is very productive.

The Summer Bergamot is a nice green pear, inclining to russet, of small size, juicy, sweet, and well flavoured, and an abundant bearer. It is round, rather flattened at both ends, with a small closed eye in a very shallow basin; the stalk is short and thick, and is also inserted in a small cavity. It is ripe in September, and does well either on the pear or on the quince stock.

The Cassolette, Lechefrion, or Muscativerd, is a most delicious middle-sized, roundish, yellowish-green pear, with red on the sunny side. It ripens in August and September; the flesh is crisp and tender, with sugary, musky-perfumed juice. It has an open eye in a slightly plaited basin, and a thick, short stalk, set in a small hollow.

The Green Chisel is a nice little round, green pear, ripening early in August. It has a large eye and a short stalk, straightly inserted without any hollow. The tree has a short, erect growth; it bears abundantly, and the fruit is in clusters. These are, perhaps, the best of our summer pears. If fewer kinds are wanted, the Green Chisel may be chosen as the earliest, but the Lechefrion and Jargonelle are the best kinds, especially as regards flavour.

The Madeleine, or Citron des Calmes, is a very early but a very poor pear; it ripens in July, and bears abundantly. Saint Jean is a very early little pear, said to ripen at Midsummer, and doing so in reality not much later. It, too, is little worth the attention of the private grower; but those who grow for the market are often glad of abundant bearers of early sorts. Cailot Rosat is another early pear which has the merit of being a most abundant bearer: the crop is immense, but the pear not very fine in flavour, although tolerably sweet and juicy.

As we get on to September and October, fine-flavoured pears become much more plentiful.

Beurré d'Amaulis is a nice juicy pear, and a good bearer. The fruit is yellowish-green, with russet markings, quite above the middle size, rather thick made, with an open eye in a shallow basin, and rather a short stalk set not quite straight in a very small cavity. It must be eaten when it is ready, or it loses its flavour; but it is, notwithstanding, a useful tree to have, as its pretty plentiful crop comes in conveniently after the very early kinds. It ripens in September.

Graciali, Summer Bon Crétien, or Boncrétien d'Été, ripens late in September, and is one of the earliest really fine-flavoured pears we have. It is a round, yellow-green pear, with a russet tinge, above the middle size, and full of delicious, sub-acid, highly-flavoured juice. The eye is small and prominent, in an evenly formed shallow basin. The stalk is short, and set in a very slight cavity. It will do on pear or quince stocks; and as it ripens, and so becomes liable to fall by the time of the rough winds, when they come early, it is best to keep it to a dwarf habit of growth. It is an old variety, and is apt to be delicate in unfavourable localities.

The Swan's Egg, that old-fashioned, old English pear, is worth cultivating from its nice flavour and productiveness, in spite of its very small size. It is a small round pear, greenish-yellow when ripe, with russet specks, and dull brown on the sunny side sometimes, and the tree bears regularly and abundantly, in such thick clusters, that it is called "fill basket" in some parts. It is a delicious-flavoured, sweet, juicy little pear, its thick, leathery skin being its greatest drawback. It ripens in October, will keep several weeks, and the tree has a tall, upright growth. The eye of the fruit is small, with a short calyx, prominently placed, and surrounded by a few wrinkled plaits; the stalk is of medium length, slender, and placed in a small cavity.

The Calebasse is a large pear, bossy, and almost equally thick all the way up. It is greyish-yellow, more yellow on the sunny side, and partly covered with a thin orange-grey russet. It is very sweet and juicy, but a little gritty. It ripens early in October, and will keep a fortnight or three weeks. It is often bent in the middle, the stalk is rather long, obliquely inserted under one or two knobs, and the eye is open, with a very short, acute calyx.

The Bishop's Thumb is similar in outline and colour, but smaller, and very fine in flavour, having abundance of rich, sweet juice. It ripens the end of October, and is a distinct and excellent pear.

The Brown Beurré is an old-fashioned, excellent English pear, large, long, tapering to the stalk, russety brown, with a little bright brown or red on the sunny side. It is juicy, melting, rich and excellent in flavour, is ripe in October, and will keep good for a few weeks. It is called Red Beurré, Golden Beurré, Beurré Gris, and many other names, no doubt from the colour varying much on different stocks and in different soils and situations. It is also called Beurré d'Anjou, Beurré d'Ambleuse, Beurré d'Amboise, and other names from places, denoting its extended popularity. The eye is small, in a shallow basin, the stalk of medium length, stout, and thickening obliquely into the fruit. The Brown Beurré does well on the pear or quince, but it is tender and subject to canker. It must have a sound, dry soil; it does best against a wall; and if the locality is not warm and sheltered, a south or south-east aspect suits it best. When it does well it is a very handsome, excellent pear.

The Beurré de Capiaumont is of middle size, pear-shaped, tapering to the stalk, good-flavoured, and clear cinnamon in colour, which is yellow in shade, but turns ruddy in sunshine. It is ripe the middle of October, and will keep several weeks. The eye is not sunk, and the stalk is short, inserted without any cavity. It succeeds well on the quince stock, and makes good open dwarf trees.

The Seckle is of American origin. It is a small, dull brown, or brownish-green pear, with a bright red cheek, and a delicious and peculiar flavour, unlike other pears. It ripens before the end of October, and it will not keep many days. It has a small open eye, with a short calyx, prominently placed, and the stalk is short, and obliquely fixed in a small cavity. This capital little pear is among the best of the American varieties; it is very hardy, ripens its fruit with certainty, and bears it in clusters at the ends of the branches.

Marie Louise is another very good October pear, which often comes forward gradually, and remains in use several weeks. It is a large, handsome-shaped pear, of a rich yellow colour, when ripe, and bright red on the sunny side if ripened in sunshine. The eye is open, in a rather knobby basin, and the stalk is long, and obliquely inserted in a small, uneven cavity. It is a juicy, nice-flavoured pear, bears well as a standard and will do on a north wall.

Louise Bonne is a large, pyramidal, very handsome, very hardy, and very excellent pear; it is so ready to grow in almost any locality, so fine in flavour, and so handsome to look at, that no garden should be without it. It is smooth and glossy, turning from a fine green, with dull red on one side, to yellow and crimson as it ripens. The eye is small, with a short closed calyx in a rather deep round basin, and the stalk is of medium length, set on obliquely, and often surrounded with a delicate russet spot. It ripens late in October, and keeps for many weeks. It succeeds on pear or quince stock, but in unfavourable localities it does much best on the quince. The tree has a healthy, vigorous growth on the quince, the wood is of greenish-brown, and the young shoots look powdered in their early stage: it is only in warm, light, loamy soils that it does well on the pear. It is cultivated with success in Scotland. Louise Bonne d'Avranche is the same pear.

The Duchesse d'Angoulême, often shortened into the Duchesse pear, is a fine, large, roundish, oblong pear, with an uneven, bossy surface, dull yellow, with broad russet patches when ripe, very juicy and high-flavoured, and with an agreeable perfume. The eye is deeply sunk in an irregular basin, and it has a stalk of medium length, which is rather thick, and inserted in an irregular cavity. It is a good bearer, and does well on pear or quince stock. It is particularly well adapted to the quince stock, and, when grafted on it, it bears early and with certainty. In size and appearance it is the finest of the autumn pears, and reaches a size and weight unusual in eating pears. The original tree is said to have been found wild in the forest of Armaillé, near Angers, about the year 1815.

The Napoleon is a fine, large, smooth-skinned pear, which is bright green until it is ripe, and then pale green, abundantly juicy and very nice in flavour. The eye is small and a little depressed, and the stalk short and thick, sometimes put on straight, and sometimes inserted diagonally under a curved boss. It ripens in November, and remains good many days. It is a plentiful bearer on an east or west wall, and grafted on the quince it makes a good open dwarf or standard. It also does on the pear stock.

The autumn pears must all be used within a very few weeks after they ripen. Some must be eaten up in a few days, or they become poor in flavour, and spoil; others may be in use for three weeks or a month, but it is only a question of a very few weeks; none are to be depended on for a winter supply, when various circumstances, in addition to their high price in the market, renders a store of fruit in the fruit-room doubly valuable. It is best, therefore, in planting the garden with fruit trees, to calculate the pear-eating capabilities of the family, and to provide about as many autumn-ripening pears as can be consumed without waste from the time the earliest autumn pears ripen, until as near Christmas as the later ones can be prevailed on, by a cool fruit-room and care, to keep good. If tolerably successful, the twelve sorts I have named would keep a very large family abundantly supplied as long as they last; and if the consumption be very great, there may be duplicates of Louise Bonne, and some others of the best kinds. If there be not space at command for so many autumn pears, without interfering with those which are necessary to provide a winter stock, Louise Bonne, Bishop's Thumb, Duchesse, Marie Louise, Graciali, and Swan's Egg, will form a good half-dozen, introducing a Brown Beurré if there be a warm, sheltered spot at liberty for it, and Beurré d'Amaulis, on account of its being a good go-between.

Doyenné Blanc, St. Michel, or Doyenné d'Or, is a most delicious October pear, which may be added with advantage to any collection. The fruit is round, bright yellow, with crimson on the sunny side, and cinnamon-russet markings. It is very sweet, mellow and juicy; the eye is small, with a closed calyx, in a shallow basin, and the stalk is also placed in a small cavity. It ripens the end of September, and keeps several weeks. It is capital for grafting on the quince stock, but will also do on the pear. It is much known as the White Beurré.

The time of gathering varies greatly, according to the weather and situation. Violent stormy weather, and an early break-up of the season, may often make it advisable to try the fruit with a view to forestalling the usual date of gathering, but we must on no account ever gather any which will not leave the tree readily.

Beurré d'Amaulis will be ready to gather by the middle of September. Graciali comes next, and will have to be stored a week or ten days later. The Calebasse has to be gathered in October, but will keep into November.

The Swan's Eggs require to be gathered in October, but in favourable seasons they will keep until nearly Christmas; and the Bishop's Thumb will do the same. The Brown Beurré, too, keeps several weeks: it requires gathering in October. Beurré de Capiaumont the same. The Seckle must be eaten at once, as it ripens. Marie Louise comes forward more gradually, and although it may be gathered early in October, some trees even earlier, the supply will last a good while, if stored with care. Louise Bonne must be gathered in October, but, if stored with care, some will last until nearly Christmas. The store of Duchesse d'Angoulême, gathered in October, will come forward by degrees, but they must be often looked over, and eaten to a day, as they ripen, or these fine and popular pears will have very little goodness. Napoleon, gathered and stored in October, will keep until Christmas. From the first week in October to the middle of the month, or a very few days later, is the time for gathering and storing almost all pears which have not been previously made safe, including the keeping sorts, and only a few of the latest may be allowed to hang on the trees later than that.

CHAPTER XII.

KEEPING PEARS.

THE transition from the pears which must be eaten a few days after they are gathered, to those of a more lasting kind, which may be in use for several weeks, or even for months, if put by with care, is so very gradual, that a division of them must not be considered imperative; as, for instance, some which I named in the last chapter will sometimes, if ripened under favourable circumstances, and well stored, keep until Christmas; and by the same rule Crassane may, and Beurré Clairgeau must often, be finished off in November, especially if the summer have given too much wet or too little warmth for favourable ripening.

Our winter pears are very dependent on the kind of season we get for their keeping properties and fine flavour. No artificial or natural warmth can compensate for the absence of abundance of genial sunshine; excessive heat ripens the fruit without properly developing its size or flavour; and an extremely dry, extremely wet season, or one in which the warmth and the wet come unseasonably, although there may be a good proportion of both, are all bad for the fruit. Our fruit crops must, both in goodness and quantity, depend greatly on seasons, and we can only watch and ameliorate the disadvantages of bad seasons, *as far as we can*, by careful culture.

Although first-class winter or keeping pears are not numerous, some few make up in goodness what they want in number. The very few which come into use from February onward far into the spring, must in no case be overlooked in planting the fruit garden. These come in when good fruit is very scarce, when it will command almost any price in London and other markets, and when pears of good quality are indeed a dainty dish to set before our friends. Besides these, we ought to have an abundant supply of fine-flavoured, good pears, to carry us over Christmas and the new year—a time when abundance of good fare is especially wanted.

Zéphirine Grégoire is a round, middle-sized pear, coming into use from November to February. It is smooth on the surface, a little bossy at the stalk, with a shining skin of a pale waxen yellow colour, inclining to orange on the sunny side; juicy, sweet, and rich in flavour, and with a delicate aroma something like that imparted by elder-flowers. On a heavy soil the skin is greener and russety. The eye is very small, sometimes on the surface, sometimes in a shallow basin; and the stalk is of medium length, thick, and set on without any cavity. It is a hardy tree, a good bearer, and very fit for pyramid or other training.

Crassane is a delicious pear, ripening in November, and going on until Christmas. It is a middle-sized, pear-shaped, short, thick, yellowish pear, thinly covered with reticulated grey russet; juicy, sweet, and peculiarly delicious in flavour. The eye is small, in a deep, narrow basin, and the stalk is long and slender, set in an open, shallow cavity. It does on pear or quince; it is said, I think without foundation, to do best on the pear; it is an excellent bearer, quite one of the best pears of its season, and it produces well on an east or south-east wall. To encourage this and other kinds to keep longer, it is a good plan to make three gatherings: the first a fortnight before the fruit is ripe, the next a week before, and the last when it is ripe. The gathering of ripe fruit will come in first, and the second and first gatherings will follow in succession. This progressive way of bringing the fruit forward is especially advisable after a hot summer.

There is a variegated-foliaged Crassane, which is a very ornamental tree. It is a variety of the Crassane; the fruit is similar, and the leaves are margined with pale yellow when they first come out, turning to white as they reach maturity. The tree has a slenderer growth, it is more tender than Crassane, and it will bear only against a wall, and with a warm aspect.

The Beurré Clairgeau is a splendid pear to look at; one which for size and beauty any cultivator may like to rear; but it hardly comes up to its appearance in goodness, being rather coarse. It is, however, sweet and juicy, piquant, and with an agreeable aroma. It is a very large pear-shaped pear, curving round at the stalk, smooth and shining, bright yellow, with large russety specks and patches, especially round the stalk, and glowing red on the sunny side—certainly a most taking pear. The eye is small and open, set in a shallow basin; the stalk rather short, stout, and fleshy. The pear ripens in October, and keeps good throughout November. The tree is not a rampant grower, on which account, as well as the large size of its fruit, it is well adapted for dwarf culture. It is good for pyramid or bush culture.

The Winter Nelis is a pear which no garden should be without. It is a medium-sized pear, wide in the centre, and growing smaller at both ends, of a dull green colour, with brownish-grey russet on the sunny side, but greenish-yellow when it ripens, and paler yellow when ripened on a wall. The eye is open, and slightly sunk in a narrow basin, and the stalk is rather long, set in a narrow and rather deep cavity. It is a mellow, delicious, sweet, juicy pear, with a rich, fine flavour. It is ripe in December, and is in use until the end of January or February. Other names are Nelis d'Hiver, Bonne de Malines, La bonne Malinaise, Colmar Nelis, Etonneau, Fondante de Malines, and Malinaise Cuvelier. It is a tree of peculiarly slender, elegant growth, requiring support for the branches when the crop is full, and the bark is very smooth and clean in appearance. It grows well as a standard, but in localities which are not very favourable of course the fruit is larger if the tree can have a wall. It is hardy, a moderate grower, and a good bearer; it makes a good pyramid on the quince stock, or does well for bush culture. It is scarcely of sufficiently robust habit to form large orchard trees: for that purpose it requires to be worked high up on some stronger-growing kind.

The Passe Colmar is a middle-sized, thick-made pear, rather flattened at the top, green, turning yellowish when ripe, sprinkled with russet, and, if exposed, tinged with red. It has an uneven surface, with slight longitudinal furrows from the stalk upwards. It is a juicy, rich-flavoured, nice pear, in use in December and January. It is an abundant bearer, either as a standard or on a wall; and if it have a wall, an east or south-east aspect will do.

The Beurré d'Aremberg is an excellent pear; one that no garden should be without. It is rather large, bossy in shape, largest in the middle, pale green with russet markings, changing to a yellow tinge when ripe. The fruit is particularly delicious; it is firm, juicy, sweet, free from grittiness, and very rich and excellent in flavour. It is one of our best keeping pears, and is in use from December to February. The eye is small, the stalk of medium length, strong, straight, and set in an angular cavity, but in some specimens it is set diagonally under a boss. It is also called Colmar Deschamps, and by other names. It does on pear or quince; it is most general on the quince, and it does well either as a standard or on a wall.

The Glout Morceau is another excellent and good keeping pear, similar to Beurré d'Aremberg in appearance, but larger. It is very good in flavour, but apt to be a little gritty round the core. It ripens in November, and will keep until February or March. It will grow as a standard; but, of course, better against a wall. Other names for it are Gloux Morceaux and Beurré d'Hardenpont.

The Beurré Diel is a fine large pear, thick in the middle, going off to the eye and tapering to the stalk. It is bright green, changing to orange in ripening, with a little trace of russet. The eye is close, in a deep hollow, surrounded by knobs, ribs, or thick bosses, and the stalk is long, strong, bent, and set in a deep, irregularly-angled cavity. The pear is sweet, juicy, and melting, and deliciously rich and aromatic in flavour. It keeps from November to January. It is a hardy tree, will do well as a standard, and is an abundant bearer. If it have a wall, an eastern aspect will do very well for it. Its popularity is attested by its numerous synonymes: Diel's Butterbirne, Dorothée Royale, Beurré Royale, Beurré de Gelle, and Poire de Melon.

The Chaumontelle is a fine, large, well-known, late pear, of an oblong, irregular, bossy figure, with a rough skin, varying in colour under different circumstances of ripening —yellowish-green, yellow, or cinnamon, ruddy on the sunny side, and marked with russet. It is very tender in the flesh, rich and high-flavoured, but it varies much in goodness from different circumstances, or if eaten a little too soon or a little too late. It is good from November to March; but the store should be constantly looked over with a discerning eye, to pick out those which are ready for eating. The eye is small, deeply sunk in an angular basin, and the stalk is short, set in a rather deep angular cavity. It has many names—Bezy de Chaumontelle, Beurré d'Hiver, Winter Beurré, and Oxford Chaumontelle. It is a hardy tree, grows well as a standard or espalier; but of course the fruit is finest in a warm, favourable locality. It does best when grafted on the quince stock. When the trees are planted in good soil, with a favourable aspect, the branches kept well apart, only strong spurs allowed, and the fruit abundantly thinned out, the pears reach an amazing size. In Jersey, the Chaumontelle pears form a staple product, and there are few even private gardens, the owners of which do not sell their pears for the supply of the London market.

We now come to a period of the year when fruit is scarce indeed, when pears are getting very rare and expensive, and when even our apple stores give in. There are three kinds which should be especially looked after for giving a supply from the time the Chaumontelles are used up until May, and as nearly on to June as can be: they are Easter Beurré, Beurré Rance, and Josephine de Malines.

The Easter Beurré is a splendid pear, and one that keeps almost the best of any, but unfortunately it is a most uncertain bearer. Some trees will bear fine crops of splendid fruit year after year, and others may be treated with the greatest care, and borne with for many years, but seem obstinately bent on making positively no return, yet it is so excellent where it does do well as to have many synonymes: in France it is well known as Beurré de la Pentecôte, Bergamotte de la Pentecôte, Beurré de Pâques, Beurré d'Hiver de Bruxelles, and Doyenné d'Hiver. The result of my experience of the excellence of this capital late pear, and the difficulty of getting it, is not on any account to advise cultivators to do without it, for no garden should be without it, but to take especial pains to get good, productive Easter Beurrés, and then to give them the care they deserve; mind not to plant trees from any stock unless it is known to be good and productive. In Jersey, the very land of pears, the Easter Beurré is uncertain as elsewhere. The fruit is large, and rather round, green, turning to russety-yellow in ripening, with streaks of brown on the sunny side. It is deliciously mellow, juicy, and high-flavoured, and lasts, in good order, from Christmas to May, or even June. The eye is small, in a medium-sized basin, and the stalk is short and thick, set in a deep, angled cavity. It does on the pear or on the quince; if the locality is not very favourable, it wants a south or south-east wall, but if it be pretty good it will thrive as a standard. Grafted on the quince, it is sometimes a profuse bearer, for when it does bear it bears very well. The wood of the tree is green; it prefers rather a strong soil; a poor, light one does not do for it at all. The Easter Bergamot, or Bergamotte de Pâque, is distinct from this, although similar to it in many points. It, too, is a good keeping pear.

The Beurré Rance is one of the very best late sorts we have; large, tapering to the stalk, dark green with russety specks, and deliciously rich in flavour. It is rather apt to shrivel in ripening, but is nice from December to May. The eye is small and open, with a short calyx, scarcely at all sunk, and a stalk which is rather long and slender, set on without a cavity, but sometimes inserted diagonally under a wide boss. Other names for it are Beurré Epine, Beurré de Rantz, Beurré de Flandre, and some authorities say Hardenpont de Printemps. It is a good bearer.

Josephine de Malines is another valuable keeping pear. It is a middle-sized, roundish pear, with a delicate skin, pale yellow, inclining to orange on the sunny and to green on the shady side, and delicately speckled with pale brown russet, which is a little stronger round the stalk and eye. The eye is open, with short, full calyx in a shallow basin, and the stalk is of medium length, and obliquely inserted in a small, narrow cavity. It has a peculiar hyacinth-like scent; but this and the delicacy of flesh and skin are injured if the tree is grown in a heavy cold soil. The pear is rich, sweet, and juicy, with a very fine aroma. It is a good pear for coming in late, for it lasts through the spring, and has been kept until May. The tree is hardy, a good bearer, and not a rampant grower. It does well for pyramids and dwarf bushes, and is good for training, being well furnished with buds. Mr. Rivers has grown it successfully on the Hawthorn.

I have purposely made my list of keeping pears as lengthy as that of the more generally grown autumn varieties, on account of the great value of their fruit when this is almost the only choice fruit to be had. No garden should be without Crassane, Winter Nelis, Beurré d'Aremberg, Chaumontelle, Beurré Rance, and Easter Beurré, if a good tree of this last can be had.

The latest pears may often be left on the trees until the end of October, but the exact time of gathering, experience and the season must decide. In tolerably early seasons the eighth of October is said to be *the day* for gathering Chaumontelles; but any rule of the sort must, of course, be subject to variation with varying seasons and circumstances.

CHAPTER XIII.

VARIETIES OF THE LAST CENTURY.

THE age and origin of our choicest varieties of pears is a subject of great interest. Whereas many first-class sorts have rewarded careful culture within the present century, others date back hundreds of years. The Autumn Bergamotte, a nice, familiar, and popular October pear, is said to have been known in the time of Julius Cæsar; the Easter Bergamotte, a nice late pear (distinct from Easter Beurré), was known in the reign of Elizabeth; the Summer Bon Chrétien is mentioned as far back as 1629; and the early Beurré, or Ambrosia, was brought to England from France at the time of the Restoration. The Angélique de Bordeaux (Poir Angélique of Miller) was introduced in or about 1700; the Chaumontelle was a new kind in 1760; and our Jargonelle, Virgouleuse, Winter Bon Chrétien, and many others, are mentioned as long back as 1727.

The oldest version extant of Miller's list of pears (before 1765), includes many which are still first-rate favourites; and it is so curious as a means of tracing back the origin of our fine old and new kinds, that I need no excuse for giving it entire:—

1. Little Musk pear, commonly called the Supreme.
2. Chio pear, or Little Bastard Musk.
3. Hasting, or Green Chisel.
4. Red Muscadelle, or Fairest.
5. Little Muscat.
6. Jargonelle.
7. Windsor.
8. Orange Musk.
9. Great Blanket.
10. Little Blanket.
11. Long-stalked Blanket.
12. Skinless.
13. Musk Robin.
14. Musk Drone.
15. Green Orange.
16. Cassolette. (Lechefrion.)
17. Magdalene.
18. Great Onion pear.
19. August Muscat.
20. Rose pear.
21. Perfumed pear.
22. Summer Bon Chrétien, or Good Christian.
23. Salviati.
24. Rose Water.
25. Choaky pear.
26. Russelet. (Qy. Rousselet.)
27. Prince's pear.
28. Great Mouth-Water. (Qy. is this Mouille Bouche.)
29. Summer Bergamot.
30. Autumn Bergamot.
31. Swiss Bergamot.
32. Red Butter pear.
33. The Dean's pear.
34. Long Green, or Autumn Mouth-Water.
35. White and Grey Monsieur John.
36. Flowered Muscat.
37. Vine pear.
38. Rousseline.
39. The Knave's pear.
40. Green Sugar.
41. Marquis's pear.
42. Burnt Cat, or Virgin of Xantonee.
43. Le Besidery, or Bezy d'Heri (from Heri, a forest in Bretagne, between Rennes and Nantes).
44. Crassane, or Flat Butter pear.
45. Lansac, or Dauphine.
46. Dry Martin.
47. Villain of Anjou. Tulip or Orange.
48. Large Stalk.
49. Amadot.
50. Little Lord.
51. Good Louis.
52. Colmar, Manna, or late Bergamot.
53. Winter Long Green, or Landry Wilding.
54. La Virgoule, or Virgoleuse.
55. Poire d'Ambrette, from its musky flavour, like the scent of Sweet Sultan—Ambrette in French.
56. Winter Thorn.
57. St. Germain, or unknown of La Fare: discovered on the banks of that river, in the parish of St. Germain.
58. St. Augustine.
59. Spanish Bon Chrétien.
60. Pound pear.
61. Wilding of Cassoy, a forest in Britanny, where it was discovered.

62. Lord Martin.
63. Winter Citron, or Musk Orange.
64. Winter Russelet.
65. Gate pear: discovered in Poictou, where it was much esteemed.
66. Bergamot Bugi, or Easter Bergamot.
67. Winter Bon Chrétien.
68. Catillac. (Baking.)
69. La Pastourelle.
70. Double Flowering. (Baking.)
71. St. Martial, or Poire Angélique.
72. Wilding of Chaumontelle.
73. Carmelite.
74. Union.
75. Aurate.
76. Fine Present, or St. Samson.
77. Le Rousselet de Reims.
78. Summer Thorn.
79. Egg pear: the shape of an egg.
80. Orange Tulip.
81. La Mansuette.
82. German Muscat.
83. Holland Bergamot.
84. Pear of Naples.

The figures of this list do not agree with those quoted by Dr. Lindley and others from Miller's list of later date; and, on the other hand, it includes some which are not quoted from Miller. Alas! among these once-favourites, how many there are whose names are never mentioned now: what do *we* know about these three Blankets, or the Choaky pear? but it is pleasant to hear news of that date of our splendid Chaumontelle, the Jargonelle—that welcome, early visitor—the Cassolette, the Bergamots, the Mouille Bouche, the Bon Chrétien, the Louise Bonne, Crassane, and such-like abiding favourites. The White Doyenné, Doyenné d'Or, or St. Michel, than which no pear is more delicious, appears to have been well known to Miller, and popular in his day, rather more than a hundred years ago; and he names the Black pear of Worcester, for cooking, and Lord Cheyne's pear, or the Holland Bergamot, for eating, as in use for July, if kept with care.

Those who wish to pursue this subject further than we have space or opportunity for here, may consult Parkinson, who wrote a folio volume in 1629, Miller, whose works date from the middle of the last century, Duhamel's *Traité des arbres Fruitiers*, 1768, and many other excellent works, both in English and French, from that time to the present

CHAPTER XIV.

QUINCES AND BAKING PEARS.

A few paragraphs on quinces will suffice; but as they are allied to the pear, they may as well follow after it. It is most familiar to those who delight in cultivating fine fruit, from furnishing the most popular, and I think, without question, generally the best stocks for our choice and favourite pears. But it is also, for itself, a fruit worth cultivating, if room can be spared for a tree, because stewed quinces are really very delicious, much finer than any stewed pears, and for cooking in different ways, and for marmalade, they are good.

The quince may be grown from cuttings, layers, or suckers. Choose young wood for cuttings, and plant them in autumn, winter, or early spring. For layering, draw down young wood at the same time. By the following autumn, in either case, the young plants will have rooted. Suckers may be taken from quince trees on their own roots, and sorts may be propagated by grafting or budding on either quince or pear stocks.

The autumn after they are made, the young plants may be planted out in rows two feet apart, and the same distance from plant to plant, and suckers may be planted out the same.

As time goes on, train the young trees in any way required. If for standards, train to a stem three feet high or more, and then allow them to branch, with three or four regular, uniform branches. If for dwarfs, head them back near the ground, and train them for espaliers or dwarf standards.

When they have formed good heads, plant them out finally, either in the garden or orchard, or by the side of water.

To make quince stocks, put down layers at the time

above named, let there not be more than two eyes brought above ground, and when those shoot and grow five or six inches long, cut one off clean, and leave the other to form the plant. This by the next autumn should be three feet high. Plant them out in rows as soon as the leaves are off the trees, shorten them back to 18 inches, and at the end of one or two years they will be ready to graft with pears for dwarf trees. If for taller trees, they may be allowed to grow longer, and must be left to grow tall, not shortened back.

Quinces may be planted in orchards or gardens with other fruit trees. Experienced cultivators have decided that there is no danger of their injuring apples or pears by crossing.

There are four varieties.

The sweet, or apple-shaped quince, *Cydonia maliformis*, I think, is the best. A fine sort of this, ripened in the climate of Constantinople, is eaten as a fruit, and is much liked, although rather astringent in flavour. It is very handsome, like a large, round, somewhat flattened apple, and bright in colour.

The pear-shaped quince, *Cydonia oblonga*, is shaped like a pear, as its name denotes. It is used in pies, for marmalade, &c.; but it is not so fine in flavour as the first-named sort.

The Portugal quince, *Cydonia Lusitanica*, bears oblong fruit, which turns to a fine purple when dressed. It is juicy, not very harsh, is said to be best for marmalade, and is the sort most favoured in England now.

The Chinese quince, *Cydonia Sinensis*, bears cylindrical fruit, which is six inches long, but very gritty. It has borne in England, but it requires a wall.

The apple-shaped quince is scarce, but it may be obtained from good fruit-growers; it is very superior in flavour and appearance. The quince is worth growing, if only on account of the size and beauty of the bloom.

About one good baking-pear tree is sufficiently useful to deserve a place in every garden where room can be spared for it.

Belle de Jersey is about the largest. It is pear-shaped, a little bent in the middle, smooth dark green, with dull brown on one side, turning to red on a yellowish ground as it reaches maturity. The flesh is white, hard, gritty at the core, and too austere and astringent to eat raw, but it stews or bakes well. The eye is wide, in a deep hollow, and the stalk is of medium length, bent, and inserted in a deep angular cavity. It is more often mentioned as Uvedale's St. Germain, and other names are Union, Udale's Warden, Pickering, and Poire de Tonneau. It requires a favourable locality, or a wall, for the fruit to be fine, and it is in use from Christmas to April.

Trésor Amour, or Trésor d'Amour, is the best stewing pear to have, although less handsome in shape than Belle de Jersey, and not so large. It is, however, a fine large pear, rough in the skin, yellowish-green, and ruddy-brown on the sunny side. It is roundish, compressed at both ends, with a small eye in a wide open basin, and a stout stalk, of medium length, set in a deep cavity. It is juicy when it is ripe, less harsh than other baking pears, stews tender in a short time, and is fine in flavour and colour. The tree is said to do best on a pear stock. It is in use from December until March; after it has been kept too long it loses its flavour. It is of vigorous growth, and does well as a standard almost anywhere.

Other stewing pears are Bellissime d'Hiver, a very large, roundish sort, and less gritty than most, in use from November to April. The Black pear of Worcester, also called Parkinson's Warden, Pound pear, Livre, Gros Rateau Gris, Grande Monarque, and Groote Mogul, is a large roundish, coarse-grained pear of vigorous growth, in use from November to February. The Double-blossomed, Double fleur, or Arménie, is a handsome and highly ornamental tree, on account of its fine, large, double flowers. The fruit is small for a baking pear, roundish, and a little pinched in towards the stalk. It is green, turning to yellow when ripe, and red, or pale purple, on the sunny side; it is crisp and juicy. The eye is small, with an erect calyx, in an even, shallow basin, and the stalk is of medium length, and set in a very small cavity. It is in use from February to May, and does better on the pear than on the quince. It is sometimes variegated in foliage, when the fruit is striped with green, yellow, and red.

The Catillac is a well-known and popular pear. Large, roundish, yellow, when well matured in a warm season orange, with bright red on the sunny side. The eye is small, with a short, neat calyx, in a deep, wide, plaited hollow; the stalk is stout, curved, and set a little obliquely in a small cavity. The flesh is firm, and the fruit is in use from December until April. It grows best on the pear. The tree is handsome in growth, hardy, a very good bearer, and does well as a standard.

Chaumontelles which fall from the trees too soon for storing or using any other way, but which have nearly reached maturity, are very good for baking or stewing, and are fine and rich in colour, if the necessary means to make them so are taken in the cooking.

For having the colour good in stewed pears they should be done slowly: if several hours' slow simmering be allowed them, and they are then stood aside in the stewpan, covered close until cold, they will be fine in flavour and colour, and they have no need of the disagreeable addition of cochineal. If the fruit is stewed quickly, and turned out at once, it is very apt to be poor in colour, although some pears stew to a much finer red than others: Trésor is one of the best in this particular.

In baking pears in the skins the same rule should be observed. There is no better plan than to put a dish of pears in the oven in the evening, and leaving them in all night, and when they are soft, they will be a fine red throughout.

Quinces also require slow stewing.

There is no greater improvement to stewed pears than a little of the delicious flavour of the quince. If one quince be sliced into the liquor in which the pears are to be stewed, it will impart great richness to the flavour.

Both pears and quinces should be peeled and cored quickly, and, one by one, as they are done, dropped into the water which is to form the liquor, and which should be no more than enough barely to cover the fruit, when packed in close. Sugar and lemon-peel to taste may be added, and the liquor may be allowed to waste considerably; as the fruit gets uncovered by the wasting of the liquor, the steam will carry on the cooking process, if the stewpan is shut down as perfectly tight as it ought, and is *kept close shut.*

If there be any particular reason for wishing to graft any, either eating or baking pears, on the quince stock, which will not commonly grow well upon it, it may be made to do so by double working. Graft or bud a free growing sort on the quince, let it grow for a season or two, and then graft or bud it with the desired sort.

CHAPTER XV.

APPLES.

IF the pear is the most delicious, the apple is the most useful of fruits. In the ungenial springs of our climate pears are often lost, apples seldom: wisely blooming later, they escape the sharp spring frosts, and bring their fruit to perfection when the earlier flowering and more tender trees are stripped. The crop, too, is as lasting as it is secure, and we think the lady a poor manager who has not her store of apples to go to for winter and spring use, whether she have to purchase, or be in the more favourable case of having the opportunity of growing choice sorts in her own ground.

I say choice sorts advisedly, for who that can produce first-class fruit would tolerate inferior sorts, requiring equal attention, care, and cost at so inferior a return?

Of this most varied and useful fruit, the apple, *Pyrus malus*, no less than 1,500 varieties have been named, and about nine hundred had some time back been cultivated in the gardens of the Horticultural Society. The best soil for apples is a deep, strong, rather adhesive loam, resting on a sound, dry subsoil. In sour, wet land they never do well, so that the ground must be drained if necessary. Apples, like pears, are chiefly propagated by grafting, occasionally by budding.

Crab stocks are often raised from the kernel, but Codling and Paradise stocks by cuttings and layers. When the young stocks are sufficiently grown, shorten the tap roots, and plant them out a foot apart, in rows two and a half feet apart. In about three years they will be fit for grafting for dwarf or low training, or even, if well grown, for standards, if it be intended to form the stem from the graft. If the stock is to form the stem, it must be left to make about four years' growth, and be encouraged to a straight, upright growth. If strong stems are wanted to make orchard standards, let the side-shoots grow one year, and then only shorten them. These may be totally removed later, and the best season to do it is about midsummer, for the wounds will skin over better in the growing season than during the time of non-growth.

Get the scions cut in January or February, tie them in bundles, label them carefully, and plant the ends in the earth in a cool, damp place, safe from sun and wind. The stocks should be ready to burst the skin of the buds before they are grafted, the cut grafts will be backwarder, so that nourishment from the stocks will be waiting for them when they are ready to commence growing. The process of grafting was entered into in the fourth chapter.

The Burr-knot, Codling, and Juneating are the sorts that may best be raised from cuttings, and the young trees are less liable to canker than their parents. Take the cuttings from the horizontal branches, about eight inches long, with a bit of the old wood to each. Rub off all the buds but the top three, set them firmly in sandy loam, cover them with a glass, and give water from time to time. Shade them from hot sun; in July the glass may be taken off, and in the autumn they may be planted out.

The Doucin or Paradise stock for apples, like the quince stock for pears, is good for throwing fibrous roots near the surface of the ground, thus collecting the best nourishment for the tree, and for transmitting moderate growth and great fertility to the graft, which makes the tree bear early and well. On the Continent a distinction is made between the Doucin and Paradise stocks; the Doucin is used for pyramidal, and the Paradise (too poor in growth for our climate) for dwarf-bush training, the Doucin stock being of freer growth than the Pomme de Paradis, but much less free than the crab stock. The Burr-knot is a large culinary apple, which roots very readily from cuttings. Young seedling apple trees sometimes show a surface-rooting habit: any such that have a good growth and fine, healthy foliage, deserve attention with a view to stocks.

Young apple trees that have been grafted two or three years may be removed from the nursery. If for pyramidal training, they should have straight centre stems, well furnished with buds and shoots down to the stock, if for bush training, they may branch from within a foot of the ground. Put no manure round the roots in planting them, but shake a little light, friable mould in amongst the roots, fill in the earth, and scatter a little half-rotted manure on the surface of the ground, and the same surface-dressing may be given every autumn.

Trees to be trained for standards should have not less than three, nor more than four, healthy, evenly balanced shoots, to become at a future time the main branches. At the end of a year these branches should be headed down or not, according to the growth of the tree: and as the head grows thicker, all crowding shoots should be cleared away.

Pyramids may be pruned and trained, as mentioned for pyramidal pears, and dwarf bushes must be allowed shoots enough to form an equal, regularly shaped little tree; and the same pinching back and treatment recommended for pears may be pursued with them. As the tree grows, the head should be kept well balanced, so that one side shall not be higher or more crowded in its branches than the other, and all the branches distinct and apart from each other. This regularity of growth will not be difficult to keep up, by observing in every leading shoot that is pruned the growth which is required, and cutting it accordingly back to a bud which tends towards the centre of the tree, or points outwards, not to one pointing sideways to right or left. There must never be branches enough left to crowd each other; but the tree must be kept open in the centre, to let in plenty of sun and air.

The prettiest espalier, or wall tree, is formed with a centre upright shoot, and side-shoots from it on each side, to match each other. They must be early trained to stakes, to get them to form. A wall is seldom granted to an apple tree.

Apples of a compact, upright, cypress-like habit of growth are fit for pyramids, but require horizontal training of the side branches, to admit air. Those that are horizontal and crooked in growth make good bushes. All pears on quince stocks, and apples on Doucin or Paradise stocks, will need thinning out of the fruit.

Training *en cordon horizontal* is a French fashion, and may be used as an edge to the borders. A tree on a Paradise stock, with a single stem, is set in slanting, and trained along a rod, fixed ten inches above the ground, and horizontal to it. The wire is supported by pins here and there; the end of the tree is never shortened, but the side-shoots are continually kept pinched back to three leaves all the summer. It will often grow very long, and produce fine fruit.

Pyramids of apples on crab stocks, or pears on pears, may be trained into handsome pyramidal trees, twelve or fifteen feet high. Pinching back must be carefully attended to.

The apple may be treated the same as the pear in continual pinching back to three leaves each, all except the leading shoots, throughout the summer, and cutting them later in the season, as recommended in a former chapter.

The fruit must be thinned in June, and especial care

must be taken not to allow young trees to bear too heavy crops, as that will throw them back for several years. Apples of large kinds should be allowed to mature only one on each fruit-bearing spur, but smaller sorts may have two or three.

Perhaps there is not a more beautiful tree grown than a bush-trained apple in full health and culture; and it is difficult to know which most to admire,—its free and graceful growth and fine glossy foliage, the beautiful size, variegation, and sweetness of the bloom, or the plump, mellow richness of the fruit.

Apples on stocks of a dwarf habit of growth may not grow freely enough for poor, light soils, or for very tenacious ground; some persons, too, may prefer tall trees to those of a low habit and growth. In these cases, trees on crab stocks may be chosen. When trees incline to a too luxuriant habit of growth, inducing canker, root-pruning must be resorted to.

From the refreshing piquancy of the apple, early apples are perhaps about as welcome in most families as early pears; and our lists are pretty rich in having a good many nice-flavoured dessert kinds. Six may be more than a medium-sized garden will require; for summer fruit of this description, although nice, must not be allowed to trench on the yet more valuable winter supply; from these six, however, a choice can be made.

The Juneating is about the best known and most popular summer apple—a small, green, round fruit, somewhat flattened at both ends, turning to a yellow-green when quite ripe, with a little red on the sunny side. It is a tender, yet crisp, nice-flavoured little apple, when just ready for eating; but it turns poor and mealy in a very few days. The eye is small, with a closed calyx in a wrinkled basin, and the stalk is slender, of medium length, and set in a small, narrow cavity. It is ripe the end of July and beginning of August; and as a crop does not all come forward at once, one will last from first to last about a month. The tree bears well.

The Irish Peach-apple is the best-flavoured early apple we have; white in the flesh, tender, rich, juicy, and high-flavoured. It is a very bright-coloured, beautiful-looking apple; a bright yellow-green, with a rosy cheek; large for an early apple, round, and a little flattened at the ends. The eye is nearly closed by the segments of the calyx, and the stalk is short. It is an eating apple, and is ripe in August. It is known also as the early Crofton, is a capital bearer, and will keep in use for a month.

The White Astrakan is another very nice early eating apple, ripening early in August. It is whitish-green in colour, and smooth and delicate, with a bloom upon the skin, and a rosy tint on one side. The flesh is white, sometimes transparent, crisp, tender, juicy, and very pleasant and delicate in flavour. The eye is depressed in a small hollow, and the stalk thick and very short. Other names for it are Glacé de Zélande, Transparent de Moscovie, and *Pyrus Astracanica*. It will keep above a fortnight; it is a hardy tree and a good bearer, and, as its name imports, it came originally from Russia. There is also a red Astrakan, which comes in at the same time, and is very nice also.

The Red Quarenden is a deservedly popular early apple. It is below middle size, but a little larger than the Juneating, and of a uniform deep crimson, with green dots, and sometimes green on the shady side. The flesh is tinged with green, and the apples should be eaten soon after they are gathered, when they are crisp, juicy, and pleasant in flavour. The fruit from one good tree will keep in use for six weeks. The eye has a calyx, closed by long segments, and is surrounded by little knotty protuberances; and the stalk is short, thick, and deeply inserted. It ripens the middle of August, but need not be gathered until after the fruit begins to fall. It is well known as the Devonshire Quarenden; but it does not seem to be much known in that county, but rather to be popular in Somersetshire and Gloucestershire. The Sack apple is another of its names. The tree bears well, and deserves a place in any garden. There is also a White Quarenden, which ripens in ptember.

The Summer Golden Pippin deserves a place as a

handsome and excellent little eating apple. It is small and round, a little inclining to oblong, flattened at both ends. The skin is smooth, shining, and yellow, deepening to orange on the sunny side, with streaks of red. The flesh is whitish, firm, delicious in flavour, and very juicy, without perfume. The eye is wide and rather hollow, and the stalk short, inserted in a middle-sized cavity.

The Spring Grove Codlin has the advantage of being the earliest cooking apple of the year, being ready for tarts in July, and lasting until October or November. All the Codlins are similar in shape, measuring rather more in depth than in diameter, wide at the base, growing narrower towards the crown, angular at the sides, and bossy round the crown. The eye is closed by wide short segments of calyx, and is slightly sunk in a narrow, plaited basin; the stalk is short and set in a cavity, which it scarcely projects beyond. It is a greenish-yellow apple, tinged with orange on the sunny side. The flesh is sweet, with a little acid, and slightly perfumed. There are several of the Codlins that come in early. Lord Suffield also is one of the very best early cooking apples.

The following good useful kinds of cooking apples, or a few of them, will keep up the supply until after Christmas, thus economically allowing the better keeping sorts to remain until the early part of the year:—

The Old English Codlin is a well-known cooking apple, coming in usefully in the autumn, but not keeping very long. It is above the middle size, wide at the base, angular at the sides, and tapering to a comparatively narrow, bossy crown. To obtain good Codlins it is necessary to graft on a sound hedge-crab, when they form fine heads and produce good fruit; and it is then found less subject to the aphis than when the trees are grown from suckers. The Dutch Codlin is very large. The Keswick Codlin is, I believe, the five-crowned apple of some parts; the little apples may be used in tarts as soon as June, and are quite ready in August. It is such a ready and abundant bearer, that it has been much recommended to plant trees of it in cottage-gardens by owners of land.

The Hawthornden is a good cooking apple from Michaelmas to Christmas. It is generally a regularly formed, good-looking apple, rather above the middle size; but sometimes it is irregularly ridged from crown to base. It is greenish-yellow, with a blush on the sunny side, smooth, glossy skin, white flesh, and plenty of well-flavoured juice. The eye is small, set deep, with plaits round it; and the stalk is slender, rather long, and set in deep. The tree grows well, and bears near the ends of the branches, which gives it a drooping growth; it is a very good bearer.

Alfriston, or Sheppard's Seedling, is a fine large apple, green, turning to yellow tinged with orange in ripening, and with delicate russet markings. It is oblong in shape, broad at the base, becoming narrower towards the crown, and irregularly ribbed at the sides, one of the ridges being generally larger than the rest. The flesh is tinged with yellow, crisp and tender, with plenty of sweet, piquant juice. It is an excellent apple and a good bearer, coming in from October to Christmas. This is superior in flavour to both the Codlins and the Hawthornden, although they are convenient from coming earlier.

There are several good autumn eating apples from which to choose. As fine, handsome apples of large size, we have the Emperor Alexander and Beauty of Kent, kinds not to be surpassed; while, as very pretty smaller, apples, there are the Golden Pippin, Nonesuch, and Scarlet Pearmain.

The Emperor Alexander is a fine, large, roundish apple, wide at the base, and tapering to a narrow crown. It is a splendid-looking apple, greenish-yellow, with red streaks but bright red and orange, beautifully varied, on the sunny side. The flesh is tinted with yellow, crisp and tender, with a sweet, aromatic, delicious flavour. The eye is large, and deeply set in a smooth, round basin; and the stalk of medium length. It is an ornament to any garden or to any table: no garden should be without it.

The tree is a good bearer, and its fruit is a valuable eating apple from October to about Christmas. It is also called Russian Emperor, Alexander, and Aporta.

The Beauty of Kent is another splendid apple, large, and irregularly ribbed on the sides. The colour is clear yellowish-green, mottled with red, bright red and yellow on the sunny side, and with russet markings round the base. The flesh is yellowish-white, crisp and tender, and the juice plentiful and piquant. The eye is small, closed by a short calyx, and set in a narrow, angular basin; and the stalk is short and slender, and deeply set in a funnel-shaped cavity. It is a handsome and good apple, and comes in well from Michaelmas to Christmas.

The Nonesuch is a very pretty and delicious little apple, very round and regular in shape, without bosses or angles, pale yellow, spotted and marbled with orange, with streaks and patches of red on the sunny side. The flesh is white, tender, juicy, and sweet, with a slightly perfumed flavour. It is rather below the middle size, and is a handsome-looking dessert apple from Michaelmas to about Christmas. Other names are Nonesuch, and Langton Nonesuch. It is a good cooking-apple, and is one of the best kinds for making jelly. There is also a Winter Nonesuch, which is a good cooking apple; it comes in in November and keeps until March.

The Scarlet Crofton is an Irish dessert apple, similar in size and shape to the early Crofton or Irish Peach apple. The eye is wide but shallow, and the stalk short and sometimes bent. It is yellowish-russet, and red and russet on the sunny side, and the flesh is firm, crisp, juicy, sweet, and high-flavoured, and never becomes mealy. It ripens in October and lasts until Christmas.

The Golden Pippin, celebrated alike for beauty and delicacy, both of flavour and constitution, is a kind which every cultivator should possess if he can; but it is a tree which it is often difficult to procure, and which requires careful culture, a good soil, and a good situation. It is, however, worth all the care it can have.

The fruit is small and perfectly round, from one to two inches in depth and diameter; a little larger sometimes on young and comparatively vigorous trees, and smaller on old trees. The flesh is a pale bright gold colour, crisp, juicy, sweet, rich, and exceedingly delicious in flavour when we get it in perfection. The eye is small, in an even, shallow basin; and the stalk is long, for the size of the fruit, and slender. Of course the bright gold colour of the skin is very important: the gold is marked with russet specks on the sunny side, and with minute pearl-coloured specks embedded all over it. Many declare that the Golden Pippin is dying out in the country, and others consider that it may yet be procured and grown in as great perfection as ever. Lindley says, "In favourable situations, in many parts of the country, instead of the trees being in a state of rapid decay, they may be found of unusually large size, perfectly healthy, and with abundant crops of fruit, perfect in form, beautiful in colour, and excellent in quality."

The Golden Pippin must have a dry subsoil, good sound loam to grow in, and a sheltered, sunny situation, safe from the bitter blasts of spring. Where it can ripen its wood well it will thrive and keep free from decay. The tree must be cut in close, to promote a vigorous growth, and manuring with judgment will do good, while care should be taken to defend the tree from injurious insects. It does well on a wall, and deserves it. The fruit ripens in October, and will keep until after Christmas.

The Downton Pippin is a very nice little apple, rather larger than the Golden Pippin, flattened at both ends, and generally rather larger on one side than on the other, smooth-skinned and yellow, with indistinct specks all over it. The flesh is a little yellow and crisp, with brisk, rich sub-acid juice. It ripens in October or November, is a good eating apple, and will keep until Christmas. The tree is a very plentiful bearer, well calculated for supplying the market, and the fruit is a good cider apple. Other names by which it is known are Elton Pippin, Elton Golden Pippin, Knight's Pippin, and Knight's Golden Pippin.

The King of the Pippins has fruit above the middle size, rather oblong, a little wide at the base, even and regular in shape, without angles, smooth in skin, pale orange, tinged with red on the sunny side, and generally a little streaked with the same. The eye is large, and set deep in an even, very little plaited basin; and the stalk is long, slender, and half sunk in a funnel-shaped cavity. The flesh is yellow-white, firm, crisp, juicy, sweet, and full-flavoured. It is a handsome apple, nice for eating in November and December, and the tree is hardy and a good bearer. It is also called the Hampshire Yellow.

The Scarlet Pearmain, or Bell's Scarlet, is a middle-sized apple, with the conical form of the Pearmains, bright crimson on the sunny side, and a mixture of red and yellow on the other. The flesh is white, crisp, juicy, sweet, and with a rich, pleasant flavour. The eye is middle-sized, deep, surrounded by small plaits, crowned by a green calyx; and the stalk is rather long, slender, and set in deep. It is a handsome dessert apple from September to December.

The Summer Pearmain is another nice apple, of medium size, oblong, tapering gradually from the base to the crown, bright gold colour, sprinkled all over with small brown specks, and bright orange and scarlet on the sunny side. The flesh is pale yellow, firm and crisp, with a fine aromatic flavour, but not very juicy. The eye is small, with a calyx nearly closed in a wide, shallow, rather plaited basin; and the stalk is short and obliquely inserted in a knob upon the fruit. It is a capital and nice-looking eating apple, ripening in October and keeping until Christmas. It has many names, among others the Royal Pearmain, Old Pearmain, and Pearmain d'Été. In some seasons it ripens as early as September. The tree is an excellent bearer, and produces many fruit-spurs, on which account it is good for espaliers, for which it should be grafted on the Doucin stock. The branches have a slender, pretty growth.

CHAPTER XVI.

KEEPING APPLES.

WE next come to the apples which have more lengthened keeping properties, on which we depend for a supply of the most useful of all fruits until the time when we may begin to look for the return of fruit again.

The Golden Russet is a middle-sized apple, regular in outline, without angles, a little flattened at the ends, of a yellow-russet colour, rather rough and thick in the skin, and sometimes ruddy on the sunny side. The flesh is pale yellow, firm, crisp, sweet, with an aromatic, rather musky taste, and not very juicy. The eye is rather small, close, a little depressed, with irregular plaits round; and the stalk is very short, and is deeply inserted in an uneven, narrow cavity, not projecting so far as the base of the apple. It is a good-looking and nice-flavoured dessert apple from December to April, and is also excellent for cooking. The trees have a thin and rather drooping growth: they are hardy, and often bear well in bleak situations.

The Pine-Apple Russet, or Reinette Anana, is a middle-sized apple of a bright golden russet, regular in form, with the russet flavour heightened with plentiful, rich, high-flavoured juice, having something of the flavour of the pine apple. This, too, is good for either eating or cooking.

The Blenheim Orange, Woodstock Pippin, or Blenheim Pippin, is at once one of the handsomest, largest, and most useful apples we have. It is a large, roundish apple, rather widest at the base, of a bright orange colour when ripe, with a glowing rosy cheek. The flesh is yellow, breaking very juicy, sweet, and with a delicious high flavour. The eye is hollow and open, in a slightly angular cavity. It is one of the largest and handsomest of our table apples, and is also delicious for cooking. It is in use from November to March. The kind was originated at Woodstock, and it soon made its way and became deservedly very popular. No garden should be without a tree, for, in addition to the goodness of the fruit, it grows well, and is a capital bearer; so good that I have known old degenerate trees without care produce a great quantity of small fruit: its small size was, of course, in the absence of careful culture.

Reinette de Canada is another fine large apple which, on account of its goodness, no garden should be without. The fruit is large, broad, and flat, a fine greenish-yellow, a little tinged with red on the sunny side; the flesh is yellowish-white, firm and juicy, with a brisk, high-flavoured, sub-acid piquancy. The eye is rather open, with a short calyx, in a cavity surrounded with prominent ribs passing down the fruit half way; and the stalk is short, and set in a wide, open cavity. It is a good-bearing, excellent tree. The apple comes in in December and will keep until March. It is a handsome and delicious dessert apple; and it is equally good for cooking.

The Lemon Pippin is an old-fashioned but very nice apple to have. The fruit is middle-sized, oval, and regularly formed, without angles. The eye is small, open, with a short, slender calyx, and is a little depressed. The stalk is short, and growing from a knob at the end of the apple, which is yellowish-green in colour, turning to yellow in ripening, without red or russet markings. The flesh is firm, high-flavoured and pleasant, but not very juicy. This, too, is an apple which is equally nice for eating or cooking. The tree is hardy, an excellent bearer, and a very good sort for orchards. It has an erect, free, handsome growth, and the fruit is good-looking, as well as fine in flavour.

The above kinds of good keeping apples may be especially valuable in small gardens, on account of the fruit being either for eating or cooking. Some kinds are fit only for cooking.

The Golden Noble is, perhaps, the best cooking apple we have. It bakes to a soft, amber-coloured pulp, with a fine rich flavour, and just acidity enough, not too much. The fruit is large and round, becoming a little narrower towards the crown. The skin is beautifully smooth and polished, and of a fine, clear golden yellow, with just a few reddish markings and little patches of russet. The flesh is yellow, tender, and juicy, with a pleasant sub-acid flavour. The eye is small, and surrounded by little plaits, and the stalk very short and thick. It is in use from November until March. The tree is hardy and good, and bears very well.

The Wellington is another good cooking, keeping apple. The fruit is above the middle size, round, and flattened at both ends, clear yellow, with light red on the sunny side, and speckled with brown all over. The flesh is yellow and crisp, with a brisk acid flavour. The eye is large, open, and rather deeply sunk, and the stalk very short. Other names for it are Dumelow's Seedling, Duke of Wellington, and Normanton Wonder. It keeps remarkably sound and good, and is in use from November to April. The tree is a good bearer.

The Norfolk Beaufin is a kind which deserves a place in the garden, if there be room to spare. Like baking pears and quinces, it is of no use except for cooking. The fruit is above the middle size, irregular in shape, with broad angles from base to crown. The colour is deep green, with livid red nearly round the fruit, but deepest on the sunny side. The flesh is very firm, rather acid, and not juicy; but when the fruit is slowly baked, and pressed, it has a rich, fine flavour. The eye is large, in a deep basin, surrounded by irregular plaits; and the stalk not long, fleshy, and deeply set. Other names for it are Norfolk Beefin, and Read's Baker. It is in use from November to June. The tree is rather tender and apt to canker, so it requires a good soil and a warm position. The fruit, dried and pressed, is a very convenient addition to the dessert throughout the winter, and makes variety all the time that fruit is most scarce.

We may now finish up the list with a few good eating apples, which will keep until nearly the time when fruit comes round again, although some have been already mentioned among those which are good for either eating or cooking.

The Old Nonpareil is a little below the middle size, flat, and rather widest at the base, greenish-yellow when ripe, covered with pale russet, and ruddy when exposed to the sun. It eats firm and crisp, and is deliciously high-flavoured and aromatic, but not very juicy. The eye is very small and prominent, or scarcely at all depressed; and the stalk is long, slender, and standing out beyond the base of the fruit. It is a very old favourite, and has many names: the English Nonpareil, Hunt's Nonpareil, Non-paraille, Reinette Nonparaille, and Grüne Reinette. It is one of our most delicious sorts; the trees are good and regular bearers, and the fruit is in perfection from December to the end of March, but it will keep until May. To have the fruit in the highest perfection, graft it on the Doucin stock, in a good soil, and cultivate it with care. There are several other Nonpareils which are all more or less good. Braddick's Nonpareil keeps well until April, and is an abundant bearer. The Downton Nonpareil is rich in flavour, and keeps until April. The Golden Nonpareil is a handsome-looking fruit, keeping until February. The **Scarlet Nonpareil** is very handsome, and lasts until **March**; and the Pitmaston Nonpareil is excellent, and lasts until **February**.

The Calville Blanche is the most delicious of all apples in rich and peculiar delicacy of flavour: most decidedly no cultivator capable of appreciating superior first-class fruit should allow his garden to be without this excellent apple. The fruit is large, with broad, irregular ribs from the crown downwards; the skin is delicate, smooth, and polished; the colour whitish-green, turning to yellow when it ripens, and tinged with bright red on the sunny side. The flesh is white, tender, and sufficiently juicy, with a peculiarly delicate and delicious flavour. The eye is small, in a deep, angular basin; and the stalk is of medium length, slender, and deeply inserted. It is a first-rate eating apple from about Christmas until April. It is also excellent for cooking, but seems too good for that purpose. The tree grows well, and is a middling bearer. It has several other names: Bonnet Carré, Winter White Calville, and Calville Blanche d'Hiver.

The Court of Wick is a very nice little apple, which is said to have sprung from a seedling from the Golden Pippin, and is well worth cultivating. The fruit is nearly double the size of the Golden Pippin, round and regular in shape, a little flattened at both ends, greenish-yellow, but bright orange with small russet spots where exposed to the sun. The flesh is yellowish, mixed with green, crisp, tender, juicy, and high-flavoured when fully ripe. The eye is large and very open, in a shallow basin, and the stalk is short and slender. It is a very pretty dessert apple from October to April. Other names are Fry's Pippin, Golden Drop, Court de Wick, Knightwick Pippin, Phillips's Reinette, Wood's Huntingdon, and Wood's Transparent Pippin. The original tree was raised at Court de Wick, in Somersetshire, and it is quite a favourite in the West country. The trees grow well, and are hardy, bearing abundantly within the influence of the sharp blasts from the Welsh mountains, and ripening in such situations better than most kinds. It is an eating apple.

The Ribston Pippin is a splendid apple, both in beauty and flavour, which no garden should be without. It is of middle size, rather wider than deep, a little irregularly shaped, and slightly flattened at the ends. The colour is bright yellow, russety about the crown and stalk, faintly marked with red streaks round, which become deep and glowing on the sunny side. The eye is small, with a closed calyx, in a rather open, slightly plaited basin, and the stalk is short and knobby, set in a very slightly plaited cavity, and not projecting so far as the base of the fruit. The flesh is firm, crisp, tinted yellow, sweet and rich in a peculiar and delicious aromatic flavour, with just sufficient piquancy. It is a most delicious and handsome-looking dessert apple; it should be gathered in October, and will keep until March or April, but is in its greatest perfection about Christmas, or rather sooner. I do not think it is a very abundant bearer, but it is such a superior apple that no garden should be without it. So popular an apple is sure to have many names: it is called Glory of York (Ribston Hall, where the seedling was grown, is at Knaresborough, in Yorkshire), Formosa Pippin, Traver's, and Traver's Apple.

The Golden Reinette is a nice, and nice-looking apple, below the middle size, round, regular in the outline, flattened at the ends, greenish-yellow, smooth in the skin, and a little ruddy on the sunny side. The flesh is pale yellow, firm, crisp, sweet, and rich in flavour. It is a nice dessert apple from October to February. The trees grow well and bear well. This apple is popular in the London markets, and a tree of it deserves a place in the garden. Other names for it are Aurore, Yellow German Reinette, English Pippin, Kirke's Golden Pippin, and Wyker Pippin.

Supposing a garden has room for only six trees, I should choose no early apple at all, but depend on buying at the time when all fruit is comparatively cheap and good. Alfriston for cooking, and Beauty of Kent, or Emperor Alexander, and Nonesuch; or, if in a warm, favourable locality, Golden Pippin, for eating, would carry on the supply to Christmas, and three good keeping kinds might go on to the end of the season. Three better could scarcely be chosen than Blenheim Orange, Reinette de Canada, and Calville Blanche, or Ribston Pippin. If space can be found for a few others, choose Golden Noble, Beauty of Kent, and, as one good early sort, the Irish Peach Apple.

Mr. Rivers, in his useful little book, "The Miniature Fruit Garden," gives the following twenty good sorts as calculated for dwarf culture on the Paradise or Doucin stock.

KEEPING APPLES.

Twenty dessert apples, ripening from July to June, placed in the order of their ripening:—

1. White Joanneting, or Juneating.
2. Early Red Margaret.
3. Red Astrachan.
4. Early Strawberry.
5. Irish Peach.
6. Summer Golden Pippin.
7. Kerry Pippin.
8. Margil.
9. Ribston Pippin.
10. Cox's Orange Pippin.
11. Mannington Pearmain, or Mannington Golden Pippin.
12. Golden Drop (Coc's).
13. Ashmead's Kernel.
14. Old Nonpareil.
15. Reinette Van Mona.
16. Syke House Russet.
17. Keddlestone Pippin.
18. Golden Harvey.
19. Winter Peach Apple.
20. Strumner Pippin.

Mr. Rivers especially recommends Nos. 1, 5, 7, 9, 10, 12, 13, 15, and 20.

The early Red Margaret, or Red Juneating, is a nice apple, but it soon becomes mealy. The Red Astrachan is a sweet, juicy little apple, but it, too, soon becomes mealy. The Summer, or early Strawberry, ripens in September. The Kerry Pippin bears well, ripens in September, and lasts until November: it is a medium-sized apple. Margil is a nice-flavoured, small apple, keeping until after Christmas. Cox's Orange Pippin is a good sort, and lasts until February. The Pearmains are useful apples; Mannington's lasts until May. Ashmead's Kernel is a nice apple, not unlike the Old Nonpareil, and it lasts well, keeping good until May. Syke House Russet is good, and keeps until February. The Golden Harvey, or Brandy Apple, is a nice-flavoured, small apple, which keeps until about June: the tree is hardy and bears well. The Sturmer Pippin is brisk-flavoured, and keeps until June.

I will also quote Mr. Rivers's valuable list of twenty cooking apples, fit for use from July to June:—

1. Keswick Codlin.
2. Large Yellow Bough.
3. Hawthornden.
4. Cellini.
5. King of the Pippins.
6. Blenheim Pippin, or Orange.
7. Calville Blanche.
8. New Hawthornden.
9. Striped Beefin.
10. Waltham Abbey Seedling.

11. Herefordshire Pearmain.
12. Winter Pearmain.
13. Bedfordshire Foundling.
14. Greave's Pippin.
15. Dumelow's Seedling.
16. Forge Apple.
17. Rymer.
18. Baxter's Pearmain.
19. St. Sauveur.
20. Gooseberry Apple.

Mr. Rivers especially recommends Nos. 1, 3, 6, 9, 11, 13, 15, 18, 19, and 20.

Cellini is a good apple, fit to use in October. Blenheim Pippin is the same as Blenheim Orange. The Waltham Abbey Seedling is a large, handsome apple, useful from September to January. It is yellow and showy, a little like the Golden Noble. The Bedfordshire Foundling, or Cambridge Pippin, is another large, handsome apple, which keeps until March. Dumelow's Seedling is the Wellington Apple. The Forge Apple keeps until March. Rymer is a Yorkshire variety, in use in November and December: it is a good size, yellow, and good in flavour, and becomes very rich in baking. The Gooseberry Apple, or Gooseberry Pippin, is excellent for keeping, having been kept until August.

Apple trees grown as bushes are so ornamental, the fruit on them is so safe from high wind, the trees are so easy to cultivate, and the fruit so easy to gather, so completely under control, that little more need be said in their favour. None, too, who can appreciate good fruit of fine flavour should grow indifferent apples, as it must never be forgotten that trees of first-class kinds take no more room, and give no more trouble in their cultivation, than the most indifferent cider apples.

Even for cider, the best judges declare that apples of the finest sorts are best. The Golden Pippin has always in the West country been most esteemed as a cider apple. The Orange Pippin, a middle-sized, round, handsome, bright-coloured apple, is a great favourite in Herefordshire as a cider, and also as an eating apple. The flesh is yellow, and the pulp gives a fine golden tint to the cider; besides that, the fruit is excellent in flavour. The Golden Harvey, or Brandy Apple, is said to give great strength to cider, but not much richness. The Downton Pippin, and other descendants of the old Golden Pippin, are good cider apples. There are many varieties of cider apples, some of which have been known for hundreds of years.

CHAPTER XVII.

ALMONDS.

I say a few words on the almond because it is of the family of some of our choicest fruit, the peach and its varieties; but it is scarcely a tree to be cultivated in our country for its fruit, although the bitter almond in its outer covering is sometimes used for tarts. It will, with us, bring fruit to perfection on walls, in warm, sheltered spots. As an ornamental tree it is gay and beautiful at an early season, when such beauty and sweetness have double value. The almond is a native of Barbary, and is cultivated for its fruit in the south of France, Spain, Italy, and the Levant. It is propagated by budding on seedling plum stocks, and will produce if subjected to the same management as the peach.

If almonds in England produce nuts which are worth saving, they must be thoroughly dried on boards or shelves, with dry air playing over them, that they may not get mouldy when put by. They may then be stored in dry sand until they are wanted. They are nice in flavour, but I believe never so fine, nor so good, as those which are brought from abroad.

The Common Almond, *Amande commune* of French growers, is common in France, and the young trees are used as stocks for budding with peaches. The nuts are about an inch and a quarter long, with a hard, smooth shell, and a kernel which is not very fine or good.

The *Amande Douce à coque dur*, or Hard-shelled Sweet Almond, is an improved variety of it, inasmuch as the nut is larger; it is also much better for stocks for peaches, and is liked in France for that purpose. The nuts are an inch and a half long, dull in colour, and thick and hard in the shell; the kernels are small and not fine-flavoured.

The *Amande Douce à coque tendre,* or Soft-shelled Sweet Almond, is budded on the others, and is grown in the gardens in France, and eaten newly gathered in July. The kernel is sweet and nice in flavour. The shell is something like the *coque dur* in look and colour, but it is soft; one side is often flat and the other rounded.

The *Amande des Dames,* or Ladies' Almond, has a soft, light-coloured, porous shell, with a plump, rich, sweet kernel, more than an inch long. This is dried before it is eaten, and it is cultivated in the south of France as an article of commerce.

The *Amande Sultana,* or Sultana Almond, is like the Ladies' Almond, only smaller. The *Amande Pistache* is similar, but smaller still. Both these are to be found in the south of France, but they are not generally cultivated.

The *Amande Princesse* is like the *Amande des Dames,* but the shell is thinner, and rough on the surface, looking as if the outer part had been taken off.

Of the *Amande Amère,* or Bitter Almond, there are several varieties. The nuts differ in size, but they are all dark in colour, hard in the shell, and with a peculiarly fine flavour of bitter in the kernel.

CHAPTER XVIII.

APRICOTS.

IN choosing the young trees care must be taken that the stock and scion join healthily and completely; reject those in which there is an appearance of escape of sap, whether they have been grafted or budded at home, or are purchased in a nursery. The little trees should have been trained three years, or two at the least, and they should have an equal growth, a centre shoot, and not less than two from each side, of about equal thickness, length, and strength. The Brompton stock is not good, neither is the Brussels, unless to make trees for covering high walls. If you have stocks and wish to bud them, getting well-grown trees is only a work of time, and the training can be taken in hand very early. The stocks may be from the apricot or plum, or a kind of wild plum, sold for the purpose. For dwarf trees bud eight inches above the ground, for half-standards bud at three feet, and for standards at five feet.

The best soil for apricots is a good, sound, unctuous loam, with a mixture of vegetable mould, but use no manure, except on the surface, in the form of occasional mulching. Eighteen inches is sufficient depth of soil.

In warm situations far south, east and west are the aspects which often produce the finest apricots, as a hotter place is apt to make the fruit mealy; but in cooler localities, in the north, or even as far south as London, a south wall is best. In warm, sheltered localities standards may be grown, and the fruit on them is often abundant and fine in flavour; but the trees are long before they bear, and the fruit, of course, smaller.

Mr. Rivers states that the small Alberge Apricot, raised from the stone, makes a capital pyramid, producing small but highly flavoured fruit; and that the Breda also does well for the same training, if lifted or planted biennially.

An apricot may be trained as a fan, or with the branches spread out horizontally.

For training fan-like the tree should, to begin with, have a centre shoot, and two or three side-shoots on each side. Train the centre shoot straight upright, the two lowest quite horizontally, and those above them in a slanting direction.

Horizontal training is more exact and handsome in appearance. The centre branch is quite upright, and the lateral branches are perfectly horizontal, alternate, and parallel with each other.

The following winter the branches must be shortened to six inches, and they will give three shoots each, which in May or June may be trained in, six inches apart from each other; all unnecessary shoots must then be removed, and in after years the same cutting back and training in must be pursued. Pruning must be regulated by the fact that the apricot bears on the last year's shoots. The Moor Park only produces mostly on two or three years' old spurs.

The summer pruning of apricots should begin in May, by nipping off all the young shoots that point outwards, or that are irregular or misplaced. These should not on any account be torn off roughly or carelessly, but taken off with a sharp thumb-nail or knife, with a clean, neat cut, down to the branch, but not close enough to it to injure the bark. Over-vigorous shoots may be stopped in June, and so induced to put out fertile laterals.

Winter pruning had better be done when the leaves have fallen, although any time before March will do. Avoid amputation of large limbs, but cut out naked shoots, and get their places filled by good young branches. Leave a leading shoot at the end of each branch, and shorten vigorous young shoots back to the good, well-ripened wood, cutting away the unripened spray. This is done to encourage laterals for future fruiting, and to give sap to the bloom-buds. Cut off gross, out-standing spurs, but lateral spurs may be left: they sometimes produce blossom-buds, almost always doing so in the Moor Park apricot. All decayed or imperfect bits should, of course, be pruned.

The fruit should be thinned as soon as it is large enough to be used for tarts, which will be in May, or early in June. The thinning may be done twice, and, after the second time, the apricots should be about five inches apart.

Since the apricot flowers in March, and sometimes even earlier still, the bloom often wants protection, or the whole crop is lost. As much watchful care is necessary to remove protection when it is not needed as to give it when it is. Different materials have been already spoken of; and if none of them are at hand, fronds of fern, branches of spruce-fir, or wisps of straw may be used.

Although manuring to encourage a too rampant growth must be avoided, a little good mulching, when the fruit is swelling, in May, and liquid manure when it is making its last growth, will do good.

The Moor Park apricot in some localities is very subject to canker. If the tree is old, little can be done for it; in fact, when an apricot tree gets much diseased, it is generally most profitable to replace it with a young one; but canker may be prevented by taking up a young tree when it has been trained three or four years, pruning off the roots which are inclined to shoot downwards, replanting it and spreading the other roots horizontally, taking care that the part which has been budded be kept six or eight inches above the surface of the ground. The fruit should be gathered before it is quite ripe, or it becomes mealy.

The Masculine, Red Masculine, Brown Masculine, Abricot Natif Musqué, or early Masculine, is the best early apricot, ripening the middle or end of July. It was once known to ripen even in May under favourable circumstances; but the tree is tender, and requires a south or south-east aspect, and a warm, sheltered situation. If it has not these advantages the crop is not good, but if well placed it does well, and it is the earliest apricot we have. The fruit is round and small, yellow tinted, with red on one side; sweet, rather musky in flavour, and juicy. The shape is a little irregular, the suture rather deep, the stone thick and smooth, separating easily from the flesh, and bitter in the kernel. The White Masculine is similar in character.

The large early Précoce, Gros Précoce, Abricot de St. Jean, St. Jean Rouge, or Abricot Gros d'Alexandrie, ripens next. In France it is ripe at midsummer, whence its name of St. Jean. The fruit is oblong, with a deep suture, a downy, orange-coloured skin, and spots of red on the sunny side. The stone is brown, flattened oval, sharp in front, perforated along the back, and with a bitter kernel.

The Blenheim, Shipley's, or Miss Shipley's, is not so fine in flavour as the Moor Park, but it is tolerably rich, an excellent bearer, and a most useful apricot, ripening well. The fruit is oval, of medium size, and pale yellow colour. It is allied to the Moor Park.

The Hemskirke is also similar to the Moor Park in character, but it is earlier, and ripens with more certainty. It is ready the end of July or the beginning of August, and will do on an east wall. The fruit is middle-sized, roundish, rather flattened at the crown, orange and red in colour, clear orange in the flesh, tender, juicy, and peculiarly rich and delicate in flavour, like a fine greengage plum. The stone is rather small, and the kernel rather sweet.

The Breda is excellent for preserving, and the tree does well as a standard in the Southern counties. The fruit is small, inclined to be a little angular in shape, brownish-orange in colour, and rich in flavour. The stone is small, roundish, parts readily from the fruit, and the kernel is sweet, on which account this apricot is called in France *Amande Aveline*. On walls, it ripens the beginning or end of August, and lasts beyond that time on standards. It bears well as a standard, and is a capital apricot. The fruit of the Brussels apricot has a good brisk flavour; it is distinct from the Breda, especially in the kernel being bitter.

The Royal is a fine rich-flavoured apricot, which ripens in August, a week or ten days before the Moor Park. The fruit is oval, slightly compressed, dullish yellow, with a little red, a shallow suture, and orange-coloured flesh, which is sweet, juicy, and high-flavoured, with a slight degree of acidity. The stone is large, oval, blunt at the ends, detached from the flesh, and rather bitter. It is also called Royal George and Abricot Royale.

The Moor Park is the most celebrated and popular of all kinds. Other names for it are Anson's, Dunmore's, and Temple's; it is juicy, excellent in flavour, very large, and ripens the end of August or beginning of September. The fruit is large and roundish, hollow at the base, compressed at the sides, and rather larger on one side than the other. It is pale yellow, shading to orange, and marbled, with brownish-red on the sunny side, interspersed with dark specks. The flesh is orange-coloured and firm. The stone is rugged. There is a passage through the stone, which may be easily detected by passing a needle through it in at a small hole in the groove on one side, and the kernel is bitter.

No garden of choice fruit should be without the Moor Park, but the Blenheim is a fine, large, profitable tree to have, very hardy, and a certain bearer. The Orange is a good bearer, very fine for preserving, with a sweet kernel; it ripens in August. The Peach apricot is very much like the Moor Park. The Roman is most common in our gardens, popular from being hardy and a plentiful bearer; the fruit is best when not fully ripe; the kernel is bitter. The Turkey is another good variety; it has a sweet kernel. The Kaisha is a Syrian kind, which is delicious; it also has a sweet kernel; and the Musch-Musch is the sweetest of all apricots.

CHAPTER XIX.

PEACHES.

THE main requisites for peaches and nectarines are a stiff, loamy soil, and plenty of warmth and sunshine. In a season which is deficient in sunshine, our wall fruit will never be fine, however great the pains bestowed on their culture. Our late, chilly springs, too, are very detrimental to good crops in cutting off the bloom with frost, hail, or bitter biting wind, at the time the fruit should set.

These fruits, to do pretty well, *must have* a sound,

dry subsoil, and the borders for them must not be too deep, too damp, nor too rich. If the subsoil be not dry, it must be made so by draining. The bed for the trees may be two feet deep in earth, six feet wide before a wall which is about ten feet high, and eight feet wide if the wall be higher. Many good judges recommend that these borders should not be cropped; it is at any rate imperative to place upon them no deep-rooting crop, nor any that would require a degree of working of the soil which might injure the roots of the trees. If the locality be high and dry, the bed may be raised eight inches above the gravel path; if low and damp, one foot, and in very cold parts it may be yet more raised. A good, sound, slightly adhesive hazel loam is the best soil; this is a rich soil of a brown or hazel colour, from the admixture of decayed vegetable matter, and it requires no addition of manure, but a third part of good dark garden mould may be incorporated with it, and half that quantity of leaf-mould. If the subsoil is not favourable, it is best to plant on stations, as before described. The trees may have a top-dressing of manure every May.

Mr. Rivers recommends the following preparation of a peach border in light, poor localities:—Make a compost of equal parts of rotten manure and tenacious loam or clay, and spread it over the surface five inches thick, if the soil be poor and exhausted, or if it be an old garden, and four inches if the border be new, or rich with manure.

Stir the bed to the depth of two feet, mixing in the compost thoroughly. The trees may be planted during the winter, and in March, in dry weather, the border all over its surface should be thoroughly rammed down with a wooden rammer, so as to make it like a well-trodden path; some light, half-rotten manure—say from one to two inches in depth—may then be spread over it, and the operation is complete. This border must never be disturbed, except with the hoe, to destroy weeds, and, of course, never cropped: every succeeding spring, in dry weather, the ramming and dressing must be repeated, as the soil is always much loosened by frost. If this method be followed, peaches and nectarines may be made to flourish in our dry Southern counties, where they have hitherto brought nothing but disappointment. Any plan which will make wall fruit flourish on a disappointing light soil is most valuable.

Peaches and nectarines should be budded upon muscle or pear-plum stocks. The young stocks should be planted out in the nursery three feet apart, in rows four feet apart, and good, clean, healthy little trees should be chosen. The muscle stock may be budded the year after it is planted out, when the stem seldom exceeds two inches in circumference; and if it be smaller than that, so much the better. The pear-plum stocks may be budded the second year after they are planted out, as they are seldom thick enough the first year.

Most wall fruit trees are wanted for training. Choose maiden plants, or young trees which have not been cut back, and bud them in July. Put in the bud in front, pointing outwards, about six inches above the ground, and it will remain dormant until the following spring. Then cut off the head of the stock close above the bud, taking care that the cut is made clean, and slanting from the front towards the back. Some gardeners paint over the cut with white lead, or similar mixture, to exclude wet and air. During the summer the bud will produce a long shoot. The following spring it must be cut back to five or six inches long, leaving five or seven eyes. This summer the shoots must be carefully trained, and kept free from insects, and in the autumn the tree may be planted against a wall, in the place where it is to remain. If preferred, the stock may be planted against the wall before it is budded.

The Americans are said to use stocks raised from the peach-stone; but their trees do not appear to be lasting. The stones may be dried and sown in the autumn, either with or without heat. When they shoot, care must be taken to preserve them from the mice; and when the young trees are pretty well grown, they may be planted out, and their after-treatment must be the same as that of other stocks.

In the management of peach and nectarine trees, the important thing to be held in view is to keep up a constant succession of young wood all over the tree.

For the winter pruning, every shoot should be shortened in proportion to its strength, cutting back to where the wood is well ripened, which may be judged by its colour and general character. By this the pithy and unripened wood is taken away.

To do well for the tree for the following year, the best young shoots only must be spared, and they must not be left too crowded, but at a fair and regular distance each one from its neighbours. Trees which have arrived at bearing age may have the strongest bearing shoots shortened to about twelve inches in length, those of medium strength to about ten, and the weaker shoots to four or six, pruning them to a treble eye, *i.e.*, two fruit or short, thick buds, one on each side of a wood, or thin, sharp-pointed bud. Shoots which have no fruit-buds may be pruned to a wood-bud. Shoots that have been allowed to become too crowded must be thinned out. The trees should afterwards be trained, and this should be finished by February.

In pruning, always let the slanting cut be towards the wall, where it will be sheltered from sun and wet; whereas if it face forwards it looks badly, the sun cracks it, and the rain beats into it. For this reason the cut should always face backwards or downwards.

May is the time for beginning disbudding or summer pruning. With a small-bladed, sharp knife, cut off all shoots which tend forwards and backwards, except in the case of one here or there which, in spite of its awkward position, may be wanted to fill a vacancy; and take care not to go near enough to the tree to injure it. A few of them may be left with two or three leaves each, to furnish foliage for sheltering the fruit. When the shoots grow long enough, train the leading shoots to the wall, and select a sufficient number of side-shoots, low down, on the stronger branches, and train them in also at regular distances, carefully avoiding crowding. In the centre and lower part of the tree there may be room for but one side-shoot of each branch, as well as the leading shoot, but with the strong branches near the extremities two may sometimes be trained in.

If the winter pruning have left room enough, it is a better plan to cultivate two shoots from each main shoot, one, low down, on each side, by which means a good supply of young wood can be kept up. When strong shoots throw out laterals, it may be best to shorten, not to cut them off close, as it sometimes happens that two such laterals advantageously supply the place of the centre branch, and become two fruitful branches in place of one barren one. Extraordinarily vigorous young shoots should be cut out, unless they are positively required to fill up a vacancy on the wall. In summer pruning, take care to leave no more shoots than will be wanted as young wood for the next year: all crowded growth and interlacing of redundancies are mischievous.

To prevent injury from wind, nail in all the shoots which are intended to remain as soon as they are about six inches long, and continue to do so from time to time, as needful.

It is advantageous to disbud or pinch in at separate times; first in May, pinching or cutting off front and back shoots. A few weeks later, most of the apparently useless shoots may go; and a little later still, the last pinching may be attended to with discriminating selection, sparing a good allowance of the lowest-placed, young, healthy shoots, as likely to carry on a succession of bearing wood. All the disbudding should be completed by about midsummer.

Protection of the bloom has been already spoken of in Chapters VII. and XVII. It is generally required in our climate.

Thinning the fruit is necessary in all but very bad seasons indeed. It is best done at several times, and it must be managed with great caution, not to disturb, in the slightest degree, the fruit which remains, and also not to thin out too liberally at one time; for it sometimes happens, after an over-liberal thinning, that accident clears the rest of the crop. The first thinning may be done with care when the fruit is the size of a hazelnut, the next when it is as large as a walnut (then they are nice in tarts), and the third and last when the stone is hard.

French cultivators have divided peaches and nectarines into four classes:—*Pêches*, with downy skins, and flesh separating easily from the stone; *Pavies*, with downy skins, and flesh adhering to the stone; *Pêches violettes*, with smooth skins, and flesh separating from the stone; and *Brugnons*, with smooth skins, and flesh adhering to the stone: the two first we call peaches, the two last nectarines. English cultivators have made more elaborate divisions, but to enter into them would be of little use to the cultivator on a small scale.

Peaches may be grown as standards in warm localities, well sheltered from east and strong westerly winds; the fruit often ripens tolerably, and is very nice in flavour.

CHAPTER XX.

VARIETIES OF PEACHES.

A SELECTION may be made for keeping up a supply from August until the end of October, or even rather later.

Early Anne is a sweet, juicy, well-flavoured peach, a little musky, round, and rather below the middle size. It is whitish, with a little colour on the sunny side, and the flesh is tender, melting, and white to the stone, from which it separates readily. The leaves are doubly serrated, and without glands; and the bloom is large and very pale in colour. It is ripe the beginning and middle of August, and it will do on an east wall. Another name for it is White Avant.

The Early York is an excellent early peach; the fruit s greenish-white, and it is in use from the beginning to the end of August.

Acton Scot is a handsome and excellent peach. Although the fruit is rather below the middle size, it is sweet and pretty good in flavour. The fruit is narrowed and depressed at the apex, rather woolly in the skin, pale yellow, with mottling of bright red on the sunny side, and the flesh is melting, and yellowish-white to the stone, from which it separates readily. It is fuller on one side than on the other, and the suture is shallow. It is ripe the end of August and beginning of September. It is said to have been raised from Noblesse, crossed with Red Nutmeg, a small, hardy, very early peach.

Early Admirable is scarcely well named *early*, as it is less early than some others. The fruit is nearly round, above the middle size, juicy, and well-flavoured. It is yellowish-white, with a beautiful red cheek, and the flesh is white, getting red at the stone, from which it separates easily. It usually ripens in September, but it has been known to ripen in August. The leaves are crenate, with globose glands, and the flowers pale red, and of medium size.

The Late Admirable is one of our best kinds, with large, somewhat oval fruit, which is juicy and high-flavoured, with delicate, melting, greenish-tinted flesh, turning to red near the stone, from which it separates easily. The suture is deep, the shape regular and a little depressed on the summit, where there is generally a small, pointed nipple. The colour is palish-green or yellow, with streaky red on the sunny side. The leaves are crenate, with globose glands, and the tree bears small red flowers. It is hardy, and most deserving of a place in any garden, but it does best on a south or south-east wall. Royale is another of its names.

The Grosse Mignonne is a hardy, good sort, which keeps very well. The fruit is large, hollowed at the summit, larger on one side than on the other, juicy, melting, and with a rich, pleasant flavour. The suture is of medium depth, the skin not very downy, mottled with red on a yellow ground, and deepening to a full red on the sunny side. The flesh is pale yellow, with red streaks near the stone, from which it separates freely, and the stone is small, ovate, and very rough. The leaves are crenate, with globose glands, and the flowers deep-coloured and large. It is ripe the end of August and beginning of September. The name of Mignonne is said to have been given to it by one of the kings of France on account of its excellence; others are Grimwood's Royal George, Large French Mignonne, Padley's Early Purple, Royal Kensington, Véloutée de Merlet, and Vineuse.

The Royal George is a good peach, above the medium size, round, juicy, rich, and fine-flavoured. The colour is yellowish-white, speckled with red, and deeply marbled with red on the sunny side. The suture is deep, especially near the apex, the flesh melting, yellowish-white, red round the stone, and separating from it. The stone is ovate, and slightly furrowed, the leaves of the tree doubly serrated, without glands, and the flowers small. It is ripe the end of August and beginning of September, and should have a place in every garden. Other names by which it is known are Millet's Mignonne, French Chancellor, and Early Royal George. It is a good sort for forcing, but in cold, wet seasons it is subject to mildew, and should therefore be planted on a dry soil, in a warm, sheltered spot. It is inaccurately called Red Magdalen.

Barrington is an excellent, rather large, and very handsome peach, a little elongated in form, and somewhat pointed at the summit. It is melting, juicy, and very rich in flavour. The colour is pale yellowish-green, turning to deep marbled red on the sunny side. The suture is moderately deep along one side, and the flesh is yellowish-white, a little streaked with crimson round the stone. The stone parts from the flesh, and is of medium size, ovate, with a sharp point; it is very rough and dark-coloured. The fruit is ripe by the middle of September, and is very handsome in appearance. Another name for it is Buckingham Mignonne.

The Bellegarde, or Violette Hative, is a delicious peach, of very good size, round, regular, and handsome in form and appearance. It is very melting, juicy, and rich-flavoured; in colour, pale green, tinged with yellow, and deep, rich crimson on the sunny side. The flesh is pale yellow, a little streaked with red round the stone, which comes away freely, and is rather large and pointed. The suture is shallow, and the apex hollowed, with a little projecting point in the centre. The leaves are crenate, with globose glands. Like all extensive favourites, it has many synonymes, Galande, Large Violet, Early Galande, and Noire de Montreuil. It is ripe the beginning and middle of September, and it is a good sort for forcing.

Smith's Newington is a very good medium-sized peach, rather oval in shape, narrowing at the apex, and largest on one side. It is a firm, nice-flavoured peach; in colour, pale yellow or straw-coloured, with a bright dark-red cheek; and the flesh is pale yellow, turning red near the stone, to which the flesh adheres firmly. The leaves are doubly serrated, without glands, and the bloom is large and pale-coloured. Other names for it are Early Newington and Smith's Early Newington. It ripens early in September.

Noblesse is one of the best either for forcing or for the open wall. The fruit is large, rather oblong, narrower at the apex, where it has an acute nipple. It is very juicy, rich, and high-flavoured; not very downy, pale yellowish-green, but streaked and blotched with dull red towards the sun; the flesh is melting, and yellowish-white throughout. The stone is large, obovate, and pointed, and separates readily from the flesh. The leaves are doubly serrated, without glands, and the bloom is large and pale blush-coloured. It is one of our best early peaches, and ripens late in August and early in September. It is the same as Mellish's Favourite, but it differs from Vanguard, with which it is often confused, that being of a taller growth than Noblesse; the fruit, too, is more globular, with the apex depressed. The peaches are, however, of about equal merit.

Chancellor is a large oval peach, with a very distinct

suture, and a cavity at the base; it is not very downy; the colour is pale yellow, and dark crimson on the sunny side, and the flavour is very rich and fine. The flesh is yellow, turning very red round the stone. The stone is oblong, tapering to a point, and it separates from the flesh easily. It ripens the middle of September. The leaves are crenate, with reniform glands, and the flower is small and full-coloured.

The Red Magdalen is a first-rate, rather small peach, globular, but a little flattened, deeply cleft on one side, red in colour, juicy, rich and fine in flavour. The flesh is white, becoming a little red at the stone, which is blunt, rather large in proportion to the fruit, and separates readily. The leaves are doubly serrated, without glands, and the bloom large and pale-coloured. It is ripe the end of August and beginning of September. No collection should be without the real Red Magdalen: other names for it are Madeleine de Courson, Madeleine Rouge, and Rouge Paysanne.

The Royal Charlotte is another excellent sort, with fruit above the middle size, rather narrow at the apex, larger on one side than on the other, pale greenish-white, with a full deep-red cheek, juicy, rich, and fine-flavoured. The flesh is greenish-white, turning to pale red near the stone, which separates easily from the flesh. The leaves are doubly serrated, without glands, and the bloom is of medium size, and deep-coloured. It is ripe early in September. It is also called Early Purple Kew, and New Royal Charlotte.

Têton de Venus is a large peach, rather deeper than wide, with a wide deep suture from base to apex, a cavity at the base, and at the apex a broad obtuse nipple. It is sweet and excellent in flavour, pale greenish-yellow, with lively red on the sunny side, and the flesh is melting, greenish-yellow in colour, turning red at the stone, from which it separates. The leaves are deeply crenate, with globose glands, and are rather puckered on each side the midrib. The flowers are small, pale rose-coloured, edged with carmine. It is ripe the end of September.

Walberton Admirable is one of the very best late peaches, ripening the end of September and beginning of October. The fruit is pale yellow and red.

The Salway is another very excellent late variety, ripening the end of October or beginning of November. The fruit is dark orange.

These varieties, which I name suggestively, will offer sufficient choice for almost any private garden; and I think they are all kinds which may be obtained without difficulty from any good nursery. If the space be limited, it may be best to have an early and a late peach, and to choose the remainder from the best of those which ripen in September.

The Red Nutmeg, or Avant Pêche Rouge, is the earliest hardy peach of any, as it ripens the end of July. The fruit is small and sweet, with a little musky taste: it is nice-flavoured just as it ripens, but in a very little time it becomes very poor. The Malta, Belle de Paris, or Italian peach, is good and hardy: in Normandy it does well as a standard: the flavour is very excellent, and the fruit has the merit of keeping, and bearing carriage very well. It is ripe early in September. George the Fourth is a peach of American origin, which is good for forcing, and when forced it is very good in flavour. It ripens the middle of September. The monstrous Pavie of Pomponne, which has many other names, is the largest peach we have. The fruit is yellowish-white, with a very red cheek; it is not first-class in flavour. In warm, dry seasons it ripens towards the end of October, but in less favourable weather it will not ripen out of doors.

In Scotland, and cold localities, wall fruit of course requires a south or south-east wall, and in all parts which are not very warm those aspects are almost necessary. In all parts less genial than our most southerly counties, good kinds to select are Barrington, Violette Hâtive, Chancellor, Malta, Royal Charlotte, and Noblesse.

CHAPTER XXI.

VARIETIES OF NECTARINES.

The management of the nectarine is exactly like that of the peach in culture and pruning. It is perhaps the most delicious fruit of our gardens when grown and eaten in perfection; and a good succession may be kept up, with only the aid of well-placed walls, and necessary care throughout the last half of August, September, and the early part of October.

Hardwick is one of the hardiest and most prolific: the fruit is pale-greenish, and is ripe the middle and end of August.

Downton is also a good early nectarine, ripening its fruit late in August. The colour is pale green, with red on the sunny side.

The Murrey is a melting, sweet, well-flavoured nectarine of medium size, rather longer than wide, narrow at the apex, rather fuller on one side than on the other, pale green, with deep red on the sunny side, and with pale greenish-white flesh, which separates from the stone. The stone is oblong, blunt at the ends, and almost smooth. It is ripe by the end of August. The leaves are crenate, with reniform glands, and the bloom is small.

Hunt's Tawny is an excellent medium-sized nectarine, of a pale orange colour, shaded with deep red on the sunny side, and marked with russety specks. The flesh is orange-coloured, melting, delicious in flavour, and separates from the stone, which is rather blunt, and nearly smooth. The fruit is ovate, a little fuller on one side than on the other, flattened on one side, and with a prominent apex. It is early, being often ripe by the middle of August. It is said to do best budded on the pear-plum stock. The leaves are doubly serrated, without glands, and the bloom remarkably large, handsome, and deep-coloured.

VARIETIES OF NECTARINES.

The Duc du Tellier's is a very sweet, fine-flavoured nectarine, above the middle size, oblong, flattened near the suture, a little angular near the base, and narrowed at the crown or apex. It is pale green next the wall, and on the sunny side tawny, marbled with deep red or purple. The flesh is melting, greenish-white in colour, getting pink near the stone, from which it separates readily, and which is thick and blunt. The leaves are crenate, with reniform glands, and the blossom is small, of a bright pale crimson. It is ripe the end of August and beginning of September. It does best on the pear-plum stock. It is also known as Du Tellier's, Duc du Tello's, and Dutilly.

Elruge is an excellent kind. The fruit is of medium size, melting, juicy, and very delicious in flavour. It is rather longer than wide, greenish-yellow, becoming dark red or purple where exposed to the sun. The flesh is greenish-yellow, and separates from the stone. The leaves are doubly serrated, without glands, the bloom is small, and the tree an abundant bearer. Other names are Claremont, Spring Grove, and Elrouge.

The Pitmaston Orange is the best-flavoured yellow nectarine we have, good in size, sweet, juicy, and very delicious. The fruit is rather heart-shaped, wide at the base, elongated towards the crown, and ending there with an acute nipple. The skin is smooth, and the colour orange, shading to very dark red on the sunny side, mingling together where the colours meet with streaks and speckles. The flesh is melting, deep yellow in colour, with a little crimson round the stone. The stone separates easily from the flesh, and is small, sharp, narrow, and rough on the surface. This is a very valuable kind: it was named from having been raised by J. Williams, Esq., of Pitmaston, near Worcester—it is said from the Elruge. The leaves are crenate, with globose glands, and the bloom is rose-coloured, large, and beautiful. It ripens from the middle of August to the first week in September. Williams's Orange is another name.

The Violette Hâtive is a very superior nectarine, with

middle-sized fruit, broader at the base than at the apex; in colour, pale yellowish-green on the shady side, and dark red, mottled with pale brown dots, on the sunny side. The flesh is pale yellowish-green, changing to red near the stone. The stone separates readily from the flesh; it is middle-sized, roundish, and rough; the fissures on the stone are not very deep or sharp, and rays of red pass from them into the flesh. The leaves are crenate, with reniform glands, and the bloom is bright red, and small in size. This excellent nectarine ripens from the end of August to the middle of September, and it is so good that no garden ought to be without it, if by any means a bit of wall for a wall fruit tree can be found. It was of French origin, but it has long been known in England, according to Lindley, under the name of Violet simply. As Violette Hâtive it is well known to our nurserymen, and the name is much better applied than to the peach so called, although that is equally well known.

The **New White** is a nice nectarine, tender, juicy, and fine-flavoured, with a small stone, from which the flesh separates easily. It is middle-sized, such a pale, yellowish-green as to be almost white on the shady side, and tinged with red towards the sun. The leaves are crenate, with reniform glands, the blossom is large, and this nectarine does very well upon the muscle stock. It ripens the end of August and beginning of September.

The **Early Newington** is a sweet, nice-flavoured nectarine, rather below the middle size, a little flattened on one side of the suture, and fuller on the other, narrowing towards the apex, and terminating with an acute nipple. It is dark red, especially on the sunny side, and covered with a delicate bloom. The flesh is greenish-white, and red round the stone, to which it adheres firmly. The leaves are doubly serrated, without glands, and the bloom is large. It is in use the end of August and beginning of September. Several Newington nectarines are named, but there seems no reason to doubt that Early Newington, Early Black Newington,

Lucombe's Black, and Lucombe's Seedling, are exactly the same.

The Roman is a full-flavoured, excellent nectarine, very large, sometimes measuring eight inches in circumference, round in shape, a little flattened at the crown, greenish-yellow in colour near the wall, and deep purple-red on the sunny side, with russety specks, and a little roughness of skin. The flesh is firm, greenish-yellow, and turning very red at the stone, to which it adheres firmly. It is very juicy and fine-flavoured, and is ripe the beginning and middle of September. It is an old sort, having been cultivated in England more than two hundred years; and I believe it is one of our largest and best. The leaves are crenate, with reniform glands, and the bloom is large. It is also called Red Roman, and sometimes Roman Red.

The Old Newington, or Scarlet, is another good nectarine, which ripens early in September; the skin is very bright red—purple on the most coloured side.

The Peterborough, called by some growers the Vermash, is another very good green and red October nectarine. The fruit is under the middle size, and round, and the flesh is greenish-white to the stone, from which it separates. The leaves are crenate, and the bloom small, and very full-coloured. The fruit ripens early in October. To ripen well it should have a south or south-east wall, but in good seasons it is a nice little nectarine. Late Green is another of its names.

Many other good kinds could be named. Brinion, Marbled, or Violet-red-at-stone is one of the largest of the Melting sorts (to be known by the flesh separating from the stones, not adhering to them, as in the firm kinds, or clingstones). It is often as large as the Roman, and is a very good sort to have. The Tawny Newington is a very good nectarine, and the tree has a nice free growth; it, the Roman, and the Scarlet Newington are the fullest-flavoured fruit we have, especially if they are allowed to get a little shrivelled on the tree.

CHAPTER XXII.

PLUMS, AND A FEW GOOD KINDS.

PLUMS are budded or grafted generally on the Brussels stock for standards, on the common plum stock for both standards and dwarfs, and on the muscle stock for Prune Damsons, White Bullace, and some other kinds.

The Brussels stock has great vigour of growth, but not much durability. It may be cut down to the ground the year after it is planted out in the nursery, and it will, the same year, throw up a smooth fine shoot several feet high, ready for budding the following year.

More lasting trees may be made by budding on the common stock nine inches from the ground. If the stock be strong and healthy, the sort vigorous, and the soil good, it will soon grow standard high.

For standards, choose young trees which are straight and smooth in the stem, healthy, and without chafe, bruise, or any other injury, with regular heads of four equally strong, well-placed shoots. Plant them in the autumn. By the following April they will make fresh roots, and the buds will put forth; the shoots may then be cut back to three or four inches, and each will afterwards furnish three or four shoots, which will form head enough. If, when the time for the winter pruning comes round, there are not shoots enough to make a good head, the best for the purpose must be cut back again to obtain more shoots. The best of the shoots must be selected to form a good head, and they must be allowed to grow without being shortened again, unless some accident should occasion a vacancy which must be filled up. All that standard plum trees afterwards require is to look over them regularly, from time to time, throughout the year; in the summer, to carry on the disbudding process, as in other fruit trees, as far as practicable, and in the winter pruning to remove all superfluous shoots that may have been overlooked, and that may interfere with other branches, if left to grow.

Plum trees for training, either for the wall or for espaliers, should be chosen with a central upright stem, with shoots from each side, the same as other wall trees. The horizontal shoots should be trained nine inches apart, except in sorts that are of very slim growth, which may be a little closer. As in standards, the branches must be left at full length, unshortened.

For summer pruning, disbudding must be carried on (as prevention is better than cure) at intervals. First remove all the shoots which tend exactly to the front or to the back. Afterwards all gross shoots or robbers must be nipped back, preparatory to taking them out entirely, if advisable, later. A few weeks later, and finally, all shoots that are not necessary may be pruned.

For the winter pruning remove superfluous branches, and the remains of the superfluous shoots pinched back during the summer. Afterwards train the tree to the wall, as in other wall fruit trees.

Neglected plum trees, showing only a number of long naked, unproductive spurs, may be quite cut back: when the young shoots grow long enough to nail in, choose two of the best and strongest from each shortened limb, and train them in, and at the next winter's pruning cut away one of the two, and leave the other at its full length.

With plums, as with pears, there are so many of first-rate excellence that it is difficult to select a limited number; but the garden may be so planted as to keep up a succession of choice kinds from late in July to the end of October. The late kinds, such as Impératrice, Saint Catherine, Golden Drop, and all late-ripening plums, require a warm situation, and an east or south-east wall, to bring them to perfection.

Précoce de Tours is a deep purple, medium-sized plum, sweet and nice in flavour, and ripening late in July or early in August. It is covered with a bloom, the stalk is of medium length, and the flesh is brownish-yellow, with red streaks near the stone, from which it separates. It is also called Early Tours.

Jaune Hâtive is a very early plum, and deserving cultivation on that account. The fruit is pale yellow, with a little bloom, mellow but not fine in flavour, rather long-shaped, broader at the apex than at the the base, and with a suture down it. The stalk is of medium length, and slender, and the flesh yellow, and separating from the stone. On a south wall it will ripen by the middle of July, and it has been known to do so in June. It is the first plum that ripens, and is one of the oldest kinds we have, having been cultivated by John Tracdescant, the gardener of Charles the First. The branches are slender and downy. Other names for it are, Catalonian, Prune de St. Barnalé, and several besides.

Early Favourite is an excellent early plum: dark purple in the skin, fit for the table, and ripening late in July.

Early Prolific is another valuable early purple plum, good for eating, and ripening also in July.

Violette Hâtive is a sweet and pleasant-flavoured, deep violet, bloom-covered plum, rather oval, pointed at the apex, compressed towards the stalk, and with a shallow suture. The stalk is medium length, slender, and inserted in a small shallow cavity, and the flesh is green, and adheres to the stone. It ripens early in August; the branches of the tree are numerous, slender, and downy; and it is a most capital bearer. It has been cultivated in England as long as the Hâtive Jaune. Other names for it are Violet and Early Violet.

That most delicious plum, the Greengage, should be in every garden; it is almost too well known to need description. Its beautiful yellowish-green, middle-sized plums have a most exquisite, sweet, and luscious flavour. They are sometimes tinged on one side, and russety; there is a suture from the stalk to the apex; the stalk is of medium length, a little bent, and set in a small funnel-shaped cavity; and the flesh is yellowish-green, very melting, and separates only partially from the stone. It ripens the middle of August, on a standard, and earlier on a wall. The tree has smooth branches, it is hardy, and a most abundant bearer when it produces; but it is rather uncertain. It is, without exception, the best plum we have, and when grown upon a healthy standard, with plenty of sun, it is richer than when grown on a wall, although, of course, not so large. Other names are Reine Claude, Grosse Reine Claude, Dauphine, Abricot Vert, Verte Bonne, and Brugnon Greengage. There is also a Yellow Gage, which is very inferior; both are, however, excellent for preserving. Yet another, and much nearer to the Greengage in excellence, is the Purple Gage. The tree much resembles the Greengage, as does also the fruit, except in the colour, which is violet, powdered with a light-coloured bloom. It appears to be a much newer variety, and has the additional merit of keeping until October.

The Cherry plum is worth growing on account of its excellence for preserving. The fruit is small and heart-shaped, like a Bigarreau cherry, with scarcely any suture, and with a small slender prickle at the tip. It is pale red, with a few grey specks, very sweet, juicy, rather acid, and thick in the skin. The flesh is yellow and soft, adhering slightly to the stone, and the stalk is rather long and slender, set in a very small round cavity. It ripens the middle of August. The branches of the tree are smooth, with a wiry slender growth, and it is a pretty tree for shrubberies on account of the bloom coming very early. It is a good bearer, and is nice for dessert, and for tarts, as well as being so very good for preserving: it is a particularly bright-looking, pretty little plum. It is an old sort, and other names for it are Virginian Cherry, Mirabolen, and *Prunus cerasifera*. I believe it requires rather a warm position.

The Blue Perdrigon, Perdrigon Violette, Brignole Violette, or Perdrigon, is a useful plum for preserving, and also has a sweet pleasant flavour for eating. The fruit is middle-sized, oval, narrow towards the stalk, deep purple, and covered with bloom. The stalk is short, and the flesh yellow, separating from the stone. It ripens in August. The branches are downy. Of this plum Hakluyt wrote in 1582, "Of late time the plum called the Perdigevera was procured out of Italy, with two kinds more, by the Lord Cromwell after his travel." There are also the Red Perdrigon, or Perdrigon Rouge, the Violet Perdrigon, or Perdrigon Violette, and the White Perdrigon, or Perdrigon Blanc. They are all similar in character, only differing in colour, and the three last ripen rather later than the Blue. All the Perdrigons are tender as standards in England, but they do well on an east or south-east wall, or in a warm locality.

The Orleans, perhaps the best-known plum of all the kinds, is the most useful of any for common purposes, and no less excellent in flavour and abundant bearing. The fruit is of middle size, above middle size when fine; it is nearly round, often swelling rather more on one side of the suture than on the other; in colour, dark red, purplish in broad sunshine, and covered with a delicate bloom. It is very sweet and delicious in flavour, with a little astringence: the flesh is yellow, and separates clean from the stone. It is ripe the middle of August. It is also called the Red Damask; it does not appear to be an old variety, but it is mentioned by Miller. The branches are downy, and the tree is very hardy, and a constant good bearer. No garden should be without it. Wilmot's early Orleans is a much earlier plum, coming in as soon as the Précoce de Tours, *i.e.*, the end of July or the beginning of August. The branches are downy, like those of the common Orleans, and the fruit is a little larger, rather deep in the suture, and more compressed at the apex than the older one. It is also a softer and more juicy plum, and the stone is small in proportion to the size of the fruit.

The Early Orleans is much like the Orleans, but ripens about ten days earlier than it. The branches are downy, and red at the extremities.

Kirke's plum is one which every cultivator should

make room for in the garden, if he can have several varieties. The fruit is rather large, dark purple, thickly covered with bloom, which does not rub off easily, but shows a few golden specks through it, firm, rich, and juicy. It is longer than wide, broadest at the base, with a longish stalk, inserted almost without a cavity. The flesh is greenish-yellow, and separates easily from the stone, which is of medium size, oval, irregularly shaped and flattened, with a channel along one side. The branches are smooth. It is a very handsome plum, and a capital bearer, either as a standard, or on a west wall; it ripens the beginning or middle of September, coming in immediately after the Orleans. It was imported or originated, a few years ago, by Mr. Kirke of Brompton.

The Washington is a very useful plum for cooking, and is also nice for the table, being firm, sweet, and luscious. The fruit is dull yellow, with a little green, turning orange on the sunny side, with some crimson dots, and covered with a purplish bloom. It is of a good size, a little longer than wide, regularly shaped, and with a suture only at the stalk end. The stalk is rather long, and downy, and the flesh is yellow, separating easily from the stone, which is oval, blunt at the ends, and wrinkled. It is a large, handsome, and very useful plum, ripening in September. The branches are downy; it bears well as a standard, or on an east or west wall, but a south aspect is too hot for it: in such a situation the fruit degenerates. It is an American variety, as its name denotes. It is also called Franklin.

The apricot plum is one of the most delicious plums we have for preserving, on which account it deserves a place in the garden. It is also sweet and good in flavour for eating. It is rather large, round, yellow, tinged with red on the sunny side, and covered with a white bloom. The suture is deep, the stalk very short, and the flesh yellow, firm, and separating easily from the stone. It ripens the beginning and middle of September. The branches are covered with a whitish down: it is an excellent plum, and does well in a good situation; but if the spot be not favourable, it should have an east or south-east wall. It is rather an old variety, being mentioned by Duhamel, 1768, and it is also known as Abricotée, and Abricotée de Tours.

The Jefferson is an American yellow September plum, which many consider equal to the Greengage in flavour, if not superior to it, and it bears well as a standard.

The German Prune, Quetsche or Quetzen, is cultivated throughout Germany, Thuringia, Saxony, Silesia, Moravia, Bohemia, and Hungary, to dry as the prunes of commerce. The fruit is small, oblong, compressed at the stalk end, deep red or purple in colour, sweet, and slightly acid, and astringent in flavour. The stalk is of medium length, and slender, and the flesh yellow, adhering to the stone. It ripens the middle or end of September. The branches of the tree are smooth. Quetche de Brême is another name for it. The St. Martin's Quetche is a richer plum: a valuable yellow sort which hangs long on the tree, and comes into use the end of October. The Violet Diaper is another plum which is excellent when dried as a prune. It is a purple, oval-shaped plum, with a short slender stalk, rather deeply inserted; it is sweet, juicy, and pleasant in flavour, with a narrow, sharp-pointed stone. It is a fleshy, firm little plum, and ripens before the end of August. The branches are downy. In French it is the Diaprée Violette. The Brignole, Brignole Jaune, or Prune de Brignole, is a popular sort in France for drying as prunes. It takes its name from the town of Brignole, famous for its prunes, and there it is said to rank as one of the best kinds. It is a yellow plum, tinged with red on the sunny side, rather large and oval. The flesh is pale yellow and rather dry, but very sweet and good in flavour. It ripens by the end of August.

A Damson tree is well worth growing where there is room to spare for it, as it gives no trouble, and its abundant crops of agreeably flavoured fruit come in very conveniently in a family. There are several sorts of black Damsons. The Prune Damson, with small, oblong, dark-coloured plums, covered with a thick bloom, stalk of medium length, and green flesh adhering to the stone, is smart, but not rich in flavour. The Royal Damson is similar to this, but with larger fruit. Both trees have the branches downy. The Shropshire Damson has smooth branches, which are not spiny; it is said to be the best kind. To give a damson tree a fair chance, it must be grown a sound healthy standard, and planted out, uncrowded, like any other plum tree.

The Winesour is another plum that is worth growing only on account of its goodness for cooking and preserving: when preserved it is very luscious, and will keep for years. It is very like a damson, but fuller flavoured. The kind is said to have originated near Rotherham, in Yorkshire, many years back, and Rotherham is another name for it. Great quantities are preserved for the market round Wakefield and Leeds, and sent all over England.

Coe's Golden Drop is a most delicious plum, which should have a place in every garden. The fruit is very large, oval, greenish-yellow in colour, with rich red spots on the sunny side, and very sweet and fine in flavour. The suture is strongly marked, the stalk is rather long, slender, and set in a cavity, and the flesh is greenish-yellow, adhering to the stone, which is pointed. The branches are smooth, and the leaves have two globular glands at the base. It ripens the end of September, but it will hang on the tree some time after, and will keep long after it is gathered, either hung up by the stalk to a string inside a window, with a warm aspect, or each plum wrapped in soft paper, in a dry room. The original tree was raised by a market gardener, named Coe, at Bury St. Edmunds, the beginning of the present century: the Greengage and the white Magnum Bonum were the parents of this most exquisite variety. It attains its greatest perfection on an east wall, but it will do very well with a west aspect. It also bears well as a standard, and the fruit is equally excellent for the table and for preserving. Like most great favourites, it has many synonymes:—Coe's Imperial, New Golden

Drop, Coe's Plum, Bury Seedling, J. Fair's Golden Drop.

Coe's Late Red is a very good purple late plum, ripening the end of October. It is, I believe, a comparatively new introduction.

The Impératrice is another splendid, very late plum, which should have a place in every garden, however small the number of plums there is room for, provided there be an east or south-east wall to give it, which, in most localities, is necessary to bring it to perfection. The fruit is a fine deep purple, with a very thick rich bloom, oblong, blunt at the ends, and tapering a little towards the base; not very juicy, but with a sweet full luscious flavour. The stalk is very long, and the flesh firm yellowish-green, and adhering to the stone. The branches are long and smooth, and the tree is a good bearer. The fruit ripens in October, and, if well taken care of, it will keep until the middle of December. Impératrice Violette is its French name.

The Downton Impératrice was raised by Mr. Knight from the White Magnum Bonum, crossed with the pollen of the Blue Impératrice. The tree is a most rampant grower, and the young wood has much the appearance of that of the Magnum Bonum, only much stronger in its growth. The branches are long and smooth. The fruit is very much like the Impératrice in shape, but dull yellow in colour, with a very thin delicate skin, soft and mellow, with a full piquant flavour. It ripens in October, and will keep well. The White Impératrice is an earlier plum, which ripens on a west wall, but it is too delicate for a standard. The fruit is long bright yellow, with a frail bloom; transparent, firm, juicy, sweet, and separating from the stone; the stalk is short. Its French name is Impératrice Blanche, and the German Die Weisse Kaiserpflaume.

The Saint Catherine is another good old late plum, which, like the Impératrice, may be left to hang and shrivel on the tree, and acquire the richness of a sweetmeat. The plum is middle-sized, oblong, widest at the apex, with a small suture; whitish in colour, turning to pale yellow, tinted on the sunny side when it ripens, and sweet and rich in flavour. The stalk is of medium length and slender; the flesh pretty firm, yellow, and adhering to the stone. The branches are smooth. It is a good plum for preserving.

The White Bullace is worth growing if a spare corner can be found for a tree on account of its excellence and richness when preserved; the preserve will keep a year, and it is particularly luscious and fine-flavoured. The fruit is small and round, and generally grows in pairs. It is yellowish-white when ripe, a little mottled with red on the sunny side, firm and rather acid. The flavour is not very good, but it improves when the fruit hangs on the tree until frost touches it, and it is very nice for cooking. It is said to be ripe in October, but it will hang longer. The branches are slender, twiggy, and covered with down.

The above-named sorts will offer good choice for most gardens. If only six kinds could find room, I should fix on the following:—Wilmot's Early Orleans, as a good early plum, Greengage, Orleans, Apricot or Cherry plum for preserving, Coe's Golden Drop, and Impératrice, as first-rate late and keeping sorts.

I have not mentioned the Magnum Bonums, because several others are more generally useful, and more productive; but both the white and the red are fine in size and appearance, and very good for preserving and cooking. They are ripe in September. They are among our oldest kinds, having been favourites in the reign of Charles the First. The Morocco is a very good hardy early plum, which bears well as a standard, and ripens several weeks before the Orleans. It is a middle-sized, round, dark, bloom-covered plum, very nice in flavour, and will do better than most kinds in unfavourable localities. Lucombe's Nonesuch is another nice hardy plum, similar to a Greengage in appearance and flavour, but larger and handsomer, with a fine bloom, and a little variegation in colour. It ripens the same time as the Greengage.

CHAPTER XXIII.

CHERRIES.

A DEEP, mellow, rather sandy loam is the best soil for cherry trees. They will do in almost any tolerably fertile garden soil, if it be not too retentive of moisture.

Common black cherry stocks may be raised from seed. Keep the stones in sand until February, and then sow in some place which is safe from mice. In the autumn of the same year they may be planted out, two feet apart. For dwarfs, they may be budded the following year; but if they are wanted for standards, they must be allowed to remain until they have attained a sufficient height. The Mahaleb stock is best for dwarf culture, and that is usually obtained by layers; but I believe cuttings will take. Budding is safer than grafting, in avoiding the danger of escape of gum; but for dwarfs, grafting makes handsomer plants.

As cherries do well only with free open space, the stocks, when they are planted out, must be assorted, planting the tall ones for standards, and those of a low growth apart from each other, as the dwarfs would not grow well under the drip and shade of the taller.

The budded young trees should be planted where they are to remain not later than October or November, that they may have time to make fresh roots by the spring. About April, as soon as the tree begins to put out, cut it back to within three or four inches of the place where it was budded, leaving embryo shoots enough to form a good head. If more than four should put out, leave the best, and best-placed four, and rub off the remainder. Let these four grow to their full length, only cutting out superfluous shoots when they grow, to keep the head uniform and handsome. If the heads of young cherry trees are properly attended to the first three or four years, they will seldom get into a bad growth afterwards, but they will require *frequent* careful looking over

All badly placed or crowded spray growing in the middle of standards must be cut in close during the rest period, and the spurs thus left in out-of-the-way sheltered spots, although badly placed, with insufficient air and light for most seasons, may in bad seasons produce a little fruit which we should otherwise go without. All the superfluous and unruly shoots should be removed young, as the amputation of large branches must always be avoided.

Wall, espalier, and dwarf trees must be pinched in for the summer pruning. In May or June cut back all the shoots which tend in a wrong direction, except where a vacancy has to be filled, when an indifferent branch is sometimes better than none, and train in the young branches which are wanted. The distance from each other at which the branches of cherry trees are trained must be regulated by the size of the leaf. Those of a bold foliage, like the Bigarreau, must be from six to nine inches apart; and those with small leaves, like the Morello, may be closer together. The branches should be trained at their full length, horizontally. In July there may be a second summer pruning; after that there will seldom be more shoots grow that season. As the trees grow older, the spurs become longer, and must be kept within bounds by cutting them out in the winter, pruning whenever they exceed three or four inches, which will greatly improve the fruit.

Trained Morello cherry trees are best fan-shaped, training the branches diagonally. Morello cherries grow on year-old shoots, and on spurs from the older branches; but the younger the spurs are, the finer the fruit will be, so that spurs more than two years old should be cut away. The Morello produces many shoots; but they must not be left too crowded. The branches should be from three to five inches apart, training the outleaders at full length, and those which follow also. These leaders may be cut out annually in the winter pruning, and their place supplied. This will keep the tree within proper limits, and give it strength to mature fine fruit.

The cherry is an easy tree to prune, because it is not

generally of rampant growth, and it makes little breastwood. Due pinching back in summer leaves little to do in winter. The snags of young shoots shortened in summer may be further cut back, where requisite, in winter, and late-grown, immature wood may be shortened back to well-ripened wood; but very little shortening is required for bearing trees, as all which is requisite to induce the production of sufficient shoots for covering the wall should be done within the first three years after the young tree is put in its place. As in the standards, there will be some shoots to remove in the winter's pruning.

One important summer work among the cherry trees is to watch the aphides and destroy them, especially from the first warm weather until midsummer.

The usefulness of cherries need scarcely be spoken of. Morellos are excellent brandied. The Kentish cherry has the property of slipping easily from the stone, and when dried it makes a delicious confection. Many of the cherries are useful in confectionery; many most delicious for eating, and useful and good in cookery. Cherry wine is said to be nice—of that I cannot speak experimentally; but most persons appreciate the celebrated German liqueur called *Kirschwasser*, which is made from cherries.

It is difficult to keep cherries on the trees, on account of two classes of depredators, with both of which they are great favourites—the birds and the wasps. A covering of netting will keep off the birds, and with dwarf trees its application is not difficult. When preserved with nets, the May Duke may be kept in use from the time it ripens, in June, to the middle of August; the Late Duke from that time to the end of September; and Morellos to the end of October, or even later. Wasps are more difficult to deal with: to keep them off, we must cover the tree with some kind of gauzy material, not forgetting to destroy all the nests in the neighbourhood, as far as practicable.

CHAPTER XXIV.

USEFUL VARIETIES OF CHERRIES.

The garden may be so planted with cherries as to keep up a supply from the beginning of June to October.

The Early May, Small Early May, Indulle, Nain Précoce, or Cerisier Noir à Fruit Rond Précoce, is, I believe, the earliest cherry we have. It is small, round, pale red in colour, a little flattened at the stalk and crown, and tender and juicy, but not high-flavoured. The stalk is thin, not long, and deeply set. It ripens early in June, before any of the Dukes. The tree has a slender wiry growth, and small glossy leaves. It has no particular merit besides coming so early, and it is too tender to do very well as a standard, but produces well on a south or south-east wall.

Werder's Early Black Heart is a better cherry, and almost as early. The fruit is large, heart-shaped, with a deep suture on one side, dark purple, and very juicy, sweet, and rich. The stalk is stout and short, the flesh and juice are dark, and the skin is tough.

Tartarian Black, Churchill's Heart, Sheppard's Seedling, Fraser's Black, Circassian, Ronald's Black Heart, Black Russian, or Superb Circassian, is good in quality, handsome, and ripens the end of June or in July. It is heart-shaped, as some of its numerous names imply, uneven in surface, of a rich deep purple in colour, rich-flavoured, and juicy. The stone is small and rather long-shaped, and the stalk is slender and of medium length. The young shoots have an upward growth, with white epidermis, short joints, and plump leaf-buds. It produces the fruit singly, and bears well as a standard. On an east or west wall the fruit is splendid and very abundant. It well deserves a place in the garden. It appears to have been brought to England from Russia, but to have been introduced into Russia from Spain.

Knight's Early Black is another excellent black cherry, large and handsome, ripening the end of June, often ten days earlier than the May Duke. The fruit is blunt, heart-shaped, large, and uneven on the surface, like the Tartarian, deep purple when quite ripe, firm in the flesh, juicy, and full-flavoured. The stalk is long and deeply set in a round cavity. Mr. Knight raised the first tree of this kind in 1810, from the Bigarreau crossed with the May Duke. It is hardy enough to bear as a standard; but, of course, it comes earlier if it can have a south or south-east wall.

The May Duke, also known as Early Duke, and Morris's Duke, is another June cherry, when placed under sufficiently favourable circumstances to ripen it early. This most popular cherry is well known, and its roundish, deep-red fruit, rather flattened at both ends, and rich juice, saved from insipidity by a mild agreeable acid, are familiar to all lovers of cherries. The flesh is soft and juicy, the fruit grows in clusters, and the tree bears abundantly, does well as a standard, and is about the best kind for forcing. In most parts it does not ripen before the middle of July.

The Late Duke, or Anglaise Tardive, is useful from coming rather late. The fruit is larger than the May Duke, bluntly heart-shaped, a little compressed, bright glossy red, tender, juicy, and rich in flavour. The flesh is yellow and tender, and the stone rather large. This and the Archduke are very similar in character, larger in the fruit and in the foliage than the May Duke, more vigorous in growth, and spreading. They will do as standards.

The Black Heart, Guigniers à Fruit Noir of the French, Guines of Kent, or Early Black, ripens early in July, and is a very good sort. The cherries are pretty large, heart-shaped, a little flattened at the apex and on one side, with a slight suture; they are almost black when quite ripe, and the flesh is firm, mellow, and rich. The stalk is of medium length, and slender.

The young shoots of the tree have an upright growth, and are white in the epidermis; and the fruit generally grows singly.

The Black Eagle is another nice black cherry, which ripens in July. The fruit is large, flattened at both ends, deep purple or nearly black in colour, with very tender skin and flesh, and a rich full flavour. The tree is large in the foliage, and throws up very strong shoots; the fruit grows in pairs and large bunches, and the stalk is long and slender. It is a very good bearer, and does best on an east or south-east wall.

The Downton is a good white, and Büttner's Black Heart a great bearer, but not so good as the above two good black sorts.

The Elton is a fine cherry, resembling the Bigarreau, but coming earlier. The fruit is pretty large, heart-shaped, waxy yellow on the shady side, and bright red on the sunny, moderately firm, and very sweet and rich. It generally grows singly; the stalk is long and slender, and the cherries ripen in July, the same time as the May Duke. It deserves a place in every garden, and bears well as a standard, but of course is larger when it can have a wall.

Harrison's Heart is a cherry of delicious flavour. It is large, heart-shaped, yellow or amber, tinged with red on the sunny side, tender, rich, juicy, and full-flavoured. It ripens in July, and it should have an east or south-east wall.

Monstreuse de Jodoigne, Reine Hortense, Belle de Bavay, or Seize-à-la-livre, is a new kind, with many other names besides these. The fruit is of enormous size, oblong, compressed on the sides, with a thin semi-transparent skin, pale red at first, changing to bright cornelian red, and becoming darker and more brilliant as it hangs on the tree. The stalk is long and slender, and the flesh yellow, tender, juicy, with a full piquant flavour. It is ripe the middle of July, and is a fine handsome cherry.

The Royal Duke is an excellent cherry, ripening the middle of July. It is large and handsome, of a deep shining red in colour, never turning black, juicy, tender in the flesh, and rich in flavour. The stalk is of medium length.

The Bigarreau, Turkey Bigarreau, or Graffion, is deservedly one of the most popular cherries we have. It is large, irregularly heart-shaped, flattened at the stalk, pale yellow, turning amber when ripe, with glowing red on the sunny side, juicy, and delicious in flavour. The flesh is firm and yellow, and adheres a little to the stone, which is rather large and round. The stalk is long, inserted in a shallow cavity. The fruit is ripe the end of July or beginning of August. It is large and very handsome in appearance. The tree has a fine upright growth, the leaves are almost the largest of any, it throws up strong shoots, with a white epidermis, and it is a good bearer. In a warm sheltered spot it does as a standard but in a less favourable situation, it requires an east or south-east wall. The Bigarreau Napoléon is an excellent cherry, and an abundant bearer.

The Kentish is a well-known and most useful kind. Other names for it are the Flemish, Virginian May, English Weichsel, Common Red, Pie cherry, Early Richmond, and Sussex. It is of medium size, round, flattened at both ends, dingy red, a little mottled, and semi-transparent; the flesh may be called rather fleshy than firm; it is a little astringent and sweet, with an agreeable mixture of acidity. The stalk is rather short, slender, and inserted in a deepish hollow. It ripens about the middle of August; it is one of our commonest cherries, and, with the exception of the May Duke, the most hardy. The tree grows like the Morello, with slender branches and glossy leaves. The stone is fixed so firmly to the stalk that it can be drawn out with it. The cherries thus stoned, and spread out to dry, make a delicious sweatmeat, a little like Sultana raisins in appearance, which will keep in a dry place for a year or more. It is the kind of cherry most used for cooking, and I believe also for wine.

The Carnation is a fine, good-flavoured cherry, much resembling the Kentish. The fruit is large, round, flattened, thin in the skin, deep bright red, a little variegated, rather firm, juicy, with a fine brisk sub-acid flavour, gaining richness as it hangs on the tree. The stalk is a little longer than in the Kentish, and stout. It ripens the end of July and beginning of August. Other names for it are Crown, English Bearer, Nouvelle d'Angleterre, De Villeune, Rouge Pale, and Wax cherry. The tree and its branches have a very similar character to the Kentish, but with a stronger growth. The leaves are larger, and deeply and doubly serrated. It is not an abundant bearer as a standard, but produces plenty of fine fruit in a warm situation, and does very well as an espalier in a warm garden.

Florence, or Knevett's Late Bigarreau, is a heart-shaped cherry, flat at the stalk end, blunt at the apex, flattened on one side, with a shallow suture, in colour amber, marbled with pale red, and glowing red on the sunny side. It is firm, yet tender, juicy, sweet, and rich. The stalk is long and slender, set in a deep cavity. It ripens the end of July and beginning of August. It was brought to England from Florence, and succeeds best on an east or south-east wall.

The Small Black, Black Mazzard, Common Black of Buckinghamshire, Merry cherry or Merries of Cheshire, Small Wild Black, Black Polstead, or Mérisier à petit fruit, deserves some notice from being the best parent of our common cherry stocks. It grows wild in many parts, and is much cultivated in Cheshire, Buckinghamshire, and about Polstead in Suffolk. The name Merries, by which it is so often called, is from the French *Mérise:* it is the kind most used for making cherry brandy (not brandied cherries), and it is the best sort to use for stocks. The fruit is small, heart-shaped, a little flattened at the sides, without suture, with a round dimple at the apex, thin in the skin, quite black in colour, sweet, and pleasant-flavoured, but a little bitter. The stalk is rather long, very slender, set in a small round cavity, and the flesh is a deep purple. It ripens the beginning and middle of August.

The White Heart, Amber Heart, White Transparent,

Dredge's Early White, or Guignier à Fruit Blanc, is a favourite heart-shaped cherry, above middle size, dull whitish-yellow, tinged and mottled with dull red on the sunny side, melting, juicy, rich, and pleasant in flavour. The stalk is long and slender, set in a round cavity. It ripens in July and the beginning of August. The branches are slender and diverging, the epidermis is reddish-brown, and the cherries grow generally in pairs or threes.

The Morello, Milan, Cerise du Nord, Dutch Morello, Large Morello, Black Morello, Late Morello, or Ronald's Large Morello, ought to be a good useful sort, to have so many synonymes; and so it is, and a great favourite, valuable for use, and generally commanding a higher price in the market than most sorts. The fruit is large, round, dark red, becoming intensely dark when fully ripe, juicy, and full-flavoured, with a pleasant acidity. The stalk is of medium length, and the flesh is red and tender. It ripens in July and August, and is useful for cooking, preserving, and brandying; but many persons like it for the table, on account of its full piquant flavour. It was known in England considerably more than two hundred years ago. It will produce and ripen its fruit as a standard, but it requires a good position, and the crop is uncertain. As an espalier, with plenty of sun, it grows very fine, and on a north wall it bears abundantly, and the fruit ripens well, but it is less sweet than when ripened in a sunny spot. To render Morello cherries an excellent fruit for dessert, let the tree have an east, south-east, or south wall; train the branches six inches apart, or more; do not allow the fruit to be too crowded, and let them remain on the tree until they are perfectly ripe, or beginning to shrivel.

Belle Agathe has the merit of hanging on the tree very late, even until October, and it is said birds and wasps do not touch it. The fruit is a small Bigarreau, growing in clusters, heart-shaped, crimson mottled with yellow, with firm yellow flesh, and a sweet nice flavour. The stalk is of medium length.

Büttner's October Morello is the latest of all cherries. The fruit is large, round, flattened at the stalk end, and indented at the apex, reddish-brown, thin in the skin, and juicy, with a pleasant sub-acid flavour. The stalk is rather long and slender; the flesh is red, reticulated with whitish veins. It is an excellent cherry, especially for culinary purposes, and it ripens in October.

CHAPTER XXV.

GOOSEBERRIES AND CURRANTS.

A DEEP sandy loam is the soil on which gooseberries and currants do best; but they will grow and produce in any free garden soil of pretty good quality, if it be freed from superabundant moisture, and well manured. They will never do in land which retains the moisture, but they thrive the better for surface moisture during the growing period, for giving which surface-dressing is then very valuable. They generally do best in an open unshaded spot, but it is sometimes good policy to have a few *partially* shaded by trees, as they will sometimes, in severe springs, set the fruit when all on more exposed bushes is cut off.

New varieties are obtained from seed. When the fruit is ripe the seed is cleared from the pulp and sown at once. The next spring give the young plants a little bottom warmth, and they will grow up tall and strong the following summer; some may bear the second year, and all the third.

The usual mode of propagation is by cuttings or layers, generally by cuttings.

Choose for cuttings young, fine, straight, well-grown shoots, and let them be a foot or fourteen inches long, after the immature portion at the top is cut off. If only short cuttings of gooseberries can be obtained, they will strike, if they are planted under a handglass with one eye only above or even with the surface.

The month of October is the time for putting in the cuttings. All the eyes or buds except the four top ones must be cut out, as those under the earth would otherwise produce suckers. Plant them in any ordinary garden soil, in a light but not a sunny spot; put them in about four inches deep, fix them firmly in the earth, and keep them a little moist during the following spring and summer. Let them be in rows, eighteen inches apart, the cuttings being eight inches apart. Th young trees will make three or four shoots that year In the autumn cut back the shoots to about four or fiv eyes each, and by the following autumn they will be nice young bushes with six or eight shoots apiece, from which those must be chosen which are required to form the tree. In forming the bush, no shoot must be reserved except those which are well placed both as regards their direction and their distance from each other. There are seldom more than five shoots sufficiently well placed to be retained, and often only three. Leave no centre shoot: if there are three, train them triangularly; if four, let them grow in a square; and if more, regularly round an open centre, like the shape of a tulip. They may be removed to their destination at two years old, or they may remain a year longer.

Layering is done in the usual way. Raise the groun for the reception of the shoot to be layered; cut a notch below each bud, lay the shoot along, pegging it down, and putting earth over it, and every bud will grow and root.

Suckers may be taken to make bushes, but they are very apt to produce suckers themselves.

Gooseberries require free thinning for their winter pruning, and this should be done as soon as the leaves are down. A gooseberry bush must be so thinned that no shoot is within three inches of another; if they are six, nine, or twelve inches apart, so much the better, and the middle of the bush must be kept very open: attend to this especially from the very first. For the shoots to leave, choose strong ones, but not those of excessively vigorous growth. All shoots of rampant growth, poor inferior sprays, and all coarse snags in the interior, may be clean cut away. Finish up by shortening the points which are weakly, removing only the bad and spindly tips. When two or three years old spurs become too numerous they may be thinned out, leaving only young ones, which will give the fruit more room to swell.

Every year dig a trench round the bush as far from the stem as the branches spread; cut away the roots beyond, and fill it in with a compost of good loam and cow manure.

For summer culture give a top-dressing of half-rotten manure early in May. Towards the end of the time when the fruit is swelling, the points of long straggling shoots may be pinched off.

In June, much of the waste spray which chokes the centre of the bush may be removed; the grossest shoots may be cut out entirely, and those about which there is a doubt, pinched back. This will improve the fruit as well as the wood for future produce.

In the early training of young gooseberry trees, forked sticks of two kinds will be found very useful. Sticks cut from brushwood, half a yard long or so, and pointed at the end. Some must have the fork pointing downwards: these are to peg down the branches which want to grow too erect, and to draw them out so as to leave the centre of the bush open. Others must have the fork pointing upwards, and are to be used to support the branches which droop too close to the ground.

Prize gooseberries are grown on young bushes, which are kept to five or six branches each. Only two or three gooseberries are allowed to grow on each branch, and sometimes only one, and in hot weather the bushes are watered, and shaded from the sun during the hottest part of the day.

The winter pruning of currants must likewise be done as soon as the leaves are down. The side-shoots from among the spurs on the healthy, bearing branches, which have (or should have) been stopped in June, must be cut back to within an inch of the main stem, except in the case of any which may be required to fill up blanks. Shorten all the terminal points, to encourage the production of side-shoots the following summer, and to promote the formation of fruit-spurs. All the decayed wood must be cut away; but if there is much of this, the tree had better be destroyed, and a young one put to fill its place. Unless a top-dressing has been applied earlier in the year, bestow it now.

For summer culture give a top-dressing of half-rotted manure in May, three inches thick, and spread it after rain. This is especially beneficial in localities which are subject to drought. Stop or remove all the poor watery spray, and when the shoots which tend towards the centre of the bush are about nine inches long, which will be by the middle of June or so, they should be so cut back as to leave the centre open. A fortnight later all the watery, wild-looking spray round the outside of the bush may be cut back to within four inches of the base, which will leave tufts of foliage to shade the swelling fruit. Some of the side-spray on the branches may be served the same, and, if growing freely, the leading points of the shoots may be stopped also.

Currants begin to ripen in June, but will hang on the tree a long time if the birds, &c., will let them alone. White currants will hang two months, and red a good while longer. They may be saved by the bushes being covered with nets or matting. If matting is used it should be taken off once a week, on a dry, clear day, to get rid of the damp, and all the decayed leaves and currants should then be carefully picked off.

To get fine large currants, keep the trees thin of wood, as with gooseberries, and thin the spurs if they become too abundant, leaving only young ones, a few inches apart from each other.

A few white currants planted against a south wall are valuable to come in early for dessert. They may be put to fill up bare spots while other trees grow up, or, if there be wall to spare for them, they can be planted three or four feet apart. The branches should be trained six inches apart, vertically. The trees can be furnished with young wood when necessary, by cutting down every alternate limb to within a few inches of the ground, and before these grow tall, the others may be cut down; thus giving a succession of healthy, fruit-bearing branches.

Black currants are propagated in the same manner as the red and the white, and subjected to the same early training, but their habit, and the treatment they require, are somewhat different. They do best in a rather adhesive, rich moist soil, but not in a cold clay. They delight in richness, and thrive on the borders of ditches or drains.

They should be pruned as soon as the leaves are fallen, unless they are in a very rampant state of growth, in which case it is best to delay, lest they may injure themselves by putting out again. In the pruning no shortening is required, unless it be necessary to reduce troublesomely overgrown trees; but thin out liberally, allowing no two shoots to touch or cross each other throughout the tree. As they grow old or oldish, prune away old shoots entirely, and all that have merely a twig or two of young wood. The trees need not be kept so open in the centre as the red and white.

The fruit of the black currant must be gathered as soon as it is ripe, or it will drop, or shrivel and lose all goodness. It is good for cooking, for jelly, for wine, and for some other purposes, but it is a less general favourite, and less generally useful than white or red currants, or gooseberries. A small number of trees are, however, deserving of a place in the garden, especially as they will do with a north aspect, or on a shaded spot.

Gooseberries may be trained to a single stem, by removing all the lower buds until the trees are three feet high, and then allowing them to form a head. They make very attractive-looking trees, and ripen their fruit with great beauty and cleanliness. Currants, too, may be trained similarly: the branches of the head will droop over and look very graceful and pretty. Sometimes red currants are trained on a north wall, where they do pretty well, and produce; but the fruit is so very sour, that such a spot is far better devoted to Morello cherries, or almost anything else that will do in such a position.

Poor small currants are little worth growing, and should be rooted up, and their place supplied with good sorts.

For wine-making, the White Dutch is said to be the best kind, because it is the sweetest, but red currants also make as good as any British wine, provided a sufficient quantity of fruit and of sugar be allowed.

To grow currants fine, the trees must be kept very thin, and must not be allowed to produce too much fruit.

CHAPTER XXVI.

A FEW GOOD GOOSEBERRIES.

The Red Champagne, Red Turkey, or Ironmonger, is unequalled in richness. The fruit ripens rather early; it is oblong, tapering a little towards the stalk, of medium size, dark red, and hairy. The tree grows with erect branches, and is an excellent bearer. I believe Ironmonger differs from Red Champagne (although with many the sorts are reckoned the same) in having rounder and darker red fruit, a spreading habit of growth, and downy leaves. Another Turkey Red is a fine-flavoured smooth-skinned gooseberry.

The Old Rough Red, Little Red Hairy, or Old Scotch Red, is a full-flavoured small gooseberry, which is much esteemed for preserving. It is small, round, dark red, very hairy, and long in the hairs. It is one of the best, not only for jam, but for bottling green. The branches have a somewhat drooping habit of growth.

The Roaring Lion, or Great Chance, is a very large, smooth, red gooseberry. It is oblong, ripens late, the branches are inclined to droop, and it is handsome as regards size, but not first-rate in flavour.

Melling's Crown Bob is another good red. The fruit comes rather late; it is large, oblong, bright red, hairy, thin in the skin, and very good in flavour. The branches droop, and the trees bear plentifully.

Capper's Top Sawyer is an excellent red gooseberry, also ripening rather late. The fruit is large, oblong, pale red, and hairy at the stalk end. The branches are rather drooping.

Knight's Marquis of Stafford is a late, large, roundish, bright red, hairy gooseberry, very good in flavour. The branches grow rather upright.

The Red Warrington is one of the best late varieties, and Keen's seedling is equally good, and earlier. The Emperor Napoleon and Farmer's Glory are both good-bearing red sorts.

Other good red gooseberries are Diggle's Magistrate, with downy skin, and a spreading habit of growth—a first-rate kind; Miss Bold, a medium-sized, roundish, downy gooseberry, of first-rate quality and early; it resembles Red Walnut, but it is better; the bush has a spreading habit of growth; Raspberry, Old Preserver, or Nutmeg, small, thick-skinned, dark, hairy, very sweet and rich in flavour, early, and a good bearer; the bush is spreading; and Rifleman, Alcock's Duke of York, Yates's Royal Anne, or Grange's Admirable, large, roundish, hairy, first-rate in flavour, erect in growth, and a good late bearer. Rob Roy, too, is a first-rate, hairy gooseberry of medium size, and erect habit of growth. Shakspeare is large and fine-flavoured, and Small Red Globe, small, round, smooth, and of first-rate quality, with a fine sharp, rich flavour.

The Cheshire Lass is a white gooseberry, which is very useful from the fruit early attaining a fine size to use green for tarts. The fruit is large and oblong, and when it is ripe the skin is very thin, and downy. It is rich and sweet in flavour; the bush grows erect, and is a good bearer.

Cleworth's White Lion is a good white gooseberry. The fruit is roundish and downy; the tree rather of a drooping habit of growth.

The Early White is of medium size, very good, sweet, and early. The fruit is roundish, with a very thin, transparent, downy, yellowish-white skin. The bush is erect and spreading, and is an excellent bearer.

Royal White is a first-rate small, round, dessert gooseberry; the bush has an erect growth.

Crompton's Sheba Queen, a Lancashire prize kind, is a large, oblong, white, downy gooseberry, of first-rate excellence in flavour, and a good bearer. It ripens early, and the branches have an upward growth. Sheba's Queen and Whitesmith, or Lancashire Lass, are similar in character, and good bearers.

Moore's White Bear is early, large, roundish, and hairy.

Wellington's Glory is a fine-flavoured white gooseberry. It is large and roundish, with a thin, white, downy skin. The bush has an upright growth.

Abraham Newland is an excellent white gooseberry. It is large, oblong, hairy, and full-flavoured. The bush has an erect growth.

Hill's Golden Gourd is very large, oblong, greenish-yellow, and slightly hairy. It has a good flavour, and ripens early. The branches are a little drooping.

The Early Sulphur, Golden Ball, Golden Bull, or Moss's Seedling, ripens very early, and is a great bearer. The fruit is of medium size, roundish, yellow, and hairy. The bush has an upright growth, and the leaves are downy.

Rumbullion, Yellow Globe, or Round Yellow, is an excellent bearer, and the fruit is much used for bottling. It is small, roundish, pale yellow, and downy, not of first-rate flavour when ripe. The branches grow erect. There is also a green Rumbullion, similar to this except in colour. The Sulphur, or Rough Yellow, is a later gooseberry of excellent flavour, the leaves of which are not hairy.

Other good yellow gooseberries are Yellow Warrington, Yellow Champagne, or Hairy Amber, of first-rate excellence, Yellowsmith, much like it, Yellow Ball, first-rate in flavour, and Smiling Beauty, a thin-skinned, smooth gooseberry, of first-rate flavour. The White Champagne is a small white hairy gooseberry, of first-rate quality.

The Early Green Hairy, Early Green, or Green Gascoigne, is good as well as early. The fruit is small, round, deep green, and hairy, with a thin skin, and a nice sweet flavour. The bush is very erect, and is an excellent bearer.

Edward's Jolly Tar is of first-rate quality, and an excellent bearer. The fruit is large, roundish, and smooth, with yellow veins: it ripens early, and is excellent in flavour. The branches are drooping.

Massey's Heart of Oak is another good green gooseberry. The fruit is large, oblong, tapering to the stalk, green, with yellowish veins, smooth and thin in the skin. The flavour is rich and excellent, and the fruit ripens rather early. The branches droop, and the bush is an abundant bearer.

Parkinson's Laurel, Green Laurel, or Green Willow, is a large, roundish, downy, pale green gooseberry, a first-rate kind, and a good bearer. The branches grow erect; it resembles Whitesmith, and ripens rather late.

Wainwright's Ocean is a very large and rather early smooth green gooseberry. It grows with drooping branches.

Green Walnut, Belmont Green, Smooth Green, or Nonpareil, is an early kind of excellent flavour. The fruit is of medium size, oblong, dark green, and smooth, with a thin skin. The bush grows with long, spreading shoots, and the leaves are close to the branches. It is an excellent bearer.

Glenton Green, or York Seedling, is very good. It is of medium size, oblong, tapering to the stalk, green with whitish veins, very hairy, sweet and excellent in flavour. The bush has a drooping growth, and is an excellent bearer. The young shoots are downy, and prickly at the base, and the leaves are downy on the surface.

Other good green gooseberries are Jolly Anglers, a good late sort, with a downy skin, and an erect habit of growth; Gregory's Perfection, a first-rate late variety; the bush is drooping; Pitmaston Greengage, small, smooth, very sweet, and good for hanging on the tree until it becomes shrivelled; the bush grows erect; and Wistaston Hero, a hairy gooseberry of good flavour.

The premiums offered in Lancashire for new sorts of gooseberries, for many years past, have occasioned the production of an almost endless variety of this useful fruit. The prizes are given for size and flavour, and good sorts are so abundant, that it is difficult to select a few from among so many. A number of the kinds I have named are Lancashire prize kinds, but many of our older kinds are *quite* equal to them in flavour, if not in size. The Red, White, and Yellow Champagne, Rough Red, and Early Green Hairy are of the older kinds, and are unsurpassed in flavour. The price of gooseberry bushes is from 3s. to 6s. per dozen. Prize gooseberries have weighed 27 dwts. 14 grs.

CHAPTER XXVII.

VARIETIES OF CURRANTS.

Good kinds of currants may be selected with much less difficulty than gooseberries, as there has never been either scope or fancy to increase their number so extensively. The White Dutch is the best and sweetest white currant, and some bushes of it should be grown in every garden. The bunches are of a good size, the stalks and currants are yellow, and the skin rather transparent. The White Crystal is very large and white, not so sweet as the White Dutch. Many poor, small, white currants, without much sweetness, are grown which little deserve the room they occupy.

Among black currants, the Black Naples, or New Black, is by far the best, being very fine, excellent in productiveness, and milder and sweeter than any others. The bunches are short, but very numerous, and some of the currants will sometimes measure three quarters of an inch in diameter. Ogden's Black is not so large, but it too is very good, and the bush is hardier than the Black Naples. Common black currants are little worth the room they fill. The kinds of red currants are more numerous. Bushes producing poor, small, sour currants should be rooted up, and their place supplied with better kinds.

Red Dutch, Large Red, Large Red Dutch, or Red Grape, is superior in all points to the old Common Red. The bunches are long, and the currants large, deep rich red, and not acid, but sweet and rich in flavour.

Knight's Large Red is larger, and Knight's Sweet Red is sweeter; the fruit is large, but the bunches not so long, and the red paler. Knight's Early Red has no merit except that of being early.

The Cherry, or Cerise, is early, and the largest red currant we have, but it is very acid. The bunches are short, and the fruit very large and deep in colour.

La Fertile and La Hâtive are of foreign origin, and are both good sorts. La Fertile bears out its name in productiveness, and La Hâtive is early as well as good.

Raby Castle, Victoria, May's Victoria, Goliath, or Houghton Castle, is more acid than Red Dutch, but well worth growing, from its superior size, and because it is better than any other kind in hanging long on the tree. The branches are long, and the fruit large, and very bright in colour—larger and brighter than the Red Dutch. It ripens late and is a most abundant bearer.

The Champagne, Pheasant's Eye, or Couleur de Chair, is curious. The fruit is pale pink, or flesh-coloured, with red veins. The currants and the bunches are of medium size, and it is more acid than the Red Dutch.

Wilmot's Long Bunched Red is a decided improvement on Red Dutch as regards size, and it ripens rather later than it. The fruit is large and deep-coloured, and the bunches very long; said sometimes to measure over six inches in length.

Other nice red currants are Napoleon, Provence Red, Bunney's Large Red, said to be a first-rate kind, Lander's Large Red, and Gloire des Sablons.

Aphides and caterpillars are the currant bushes' worst enemies. Syringing with tobacco-water is best for getting rid of the Aphis, and hand-picking the only effectual method to use against caterpillars.

For the production of prize currants, the bushes must be cut in very close. Mr. Rivers says, "The young shoots should be annually shortened to two inches, so that the trees, when pruned, are like the stool in an osier bed. Currants make very handsome pyramids, and bear profusely."

The finest-named varieties of currant bushes may be bought for 4s. 6d. per dozen; excellent sorts may be had for 4s.; and choice new kinds are occasionally as high as 9s. the dozen.

CHAPTER XXVIII.

RASPBERRIES.

Most cultivators of a garden like to have a plantation of raspberries, because they make a delicious fruit for the table, a much-relished confection as raspberry jam, and a useful family store as raspberry vinegar— a refreshing drink in colds and fevers. The wild raspberry has been a native of woods, and so loves a damp soil, retentive of moisture. The cultivated cane follows its natural habit, and loves a moist unctuous soil, of a strong loamy character. The raspberry cane so loves moisture and richness combined, that some growers have found them thrive best planted in trenches a yard wide, and eighteen inches deep, like celery trenches, manuring the surface from time to time, to retain the damp of the summer rains. This kind of planting would not do in cold wet ground, but would be most valuable in dry, light, or poor localities. A darkish loam is generally good for them, but only good, sound garden earth will do, and the soil should be tolerably deep. A shallow soil of hot, loose sand is the worst of all for raspberries, and under any circumstances top-dressing or mulching does great good.

New plantations are made with suckers taken from the roots of the old canes, and great care must be observed to take them from a healthy stock, for if they are from those which have stood long in the ground, and are poor and lean in consequence, although there may be no positive unhealthiness, even high manuring will not make them fine without the loss of a year or two.

The suckers are drawn from the old roots by hand, with a ball of earth at the roots, if possible: a slight pull will show which are good to be removed. Any time will do for planting them between October and the middle of February. The ground for the new plantation should be deeply dug, and manured pretty liberally with half-rotten manure. The rows may be set six feet apart, and the young plants should be planted in groups of threes, four feet apart from centre to centre of each group. Early in November the young plants may be pruned: cut one strong cane to three feet, a second to two feet, and a third to within a few inches of the ground. By this method a little crop may be had the first year, and good shoots reserved for the next. Some growers, however, recommend that the young trees should be cut down this first winter to within six inches of the ground, sacrificing the first year's fruit to strengthen the canes for future years.

Seed is used to obtain new sorts. It is separated from the pulp of the fruit, dried, and put by until spring. Early in February it may be sown in a gentle hotbed. The little plants may be pricked out, in good rich mould, when they are three inches high, hardened off by the middle of May, and then planted out in the garden, in a rich bed. Afterwards train them, keep down suckers and watery spray, and when the young canes are tall, pinch off the tops to consolidate the wood.

For the culture of established canes, as soon as the year's crop is done with, cut the old bearing shoots clean away, draw the young canes a little closer together, and by the end of August pinch off the tops of the tall ones. When the leaves are off, draw out all the suckers, and prune the canes, of which about four may be left to each root. Cut these at different heights; the first about four feet high (or more if it be a very tall growing kind), the next nine inches lower, and so with all: this divides the spray and the fruit, so that none are crowded, but all get a fair share of air and sunshine. The canes may then be tied, and a top-dressing of manure may be given.

Soon after they begin to shoot in the spring, about May or so, give a slight thinning out wherever necessary, and a few weeks later, thin the suckers that are drawing on the resources of the plant and exhausting the soil. About four or five may be left to each group, choosing those which are of neither too rampant nor of a poor weakly growth. If the raspberries have not been mulched before, do it now.

The best way of training raspberries is to separate them by tying the canes, at about equal distances, round small hoops, which may be supported by light stakes or not, as necessary. It is a more general plan only to tie the tops together. Some fruit may be produced early by training the canes in the form of a fan on a south wall; raspberries may be forced either in pots, or planted in a bed in the house. They may also be forced by planting the roots outside a pit, drawing the bearing canes inside, and training them over a trellis, whilst the present year's shoots are left outside.

Raspberries produce their fruit on one-year-old wood, which when it has borne is of no more use, but may be cut down to make way for the canes of the present year, to ripen and produce fruit the next. The love of the raspberry for permanent moisture must not be forgotten in its culture. Also, although it requires a deep soil and roots deeply, encouraging the roots near the surface is as important with it as with most fruit trees, and this may be done by judicious top-dressing, and mulching. This is not a plant or tree from which we can cut a slip and graft it for propagation; propagation is from its own root, drawing on it for nourishment—an outlay that must be returned by good manuring, without which we shall never get fine fruit. The suckers produced do the parent stock no harm only provided the loss to it be compensated by plentiful manuring. Another thing with regard to the raspberry is, that it is a warmth-and-sunshine-loving plant: do not, therefore, cut off the canes straight at the top, as if one clip of the shears pruned the whole, but prune the canes to various heights, as before recommended, and thus avoid a crowded cluster of fruit and foliage, among which neither sun nor air can have fair play.

To stock the garden usefully with raspberries we may have kinds which come in before the beginning of summer, and others (or the same) to produce again in autumn.

The Red and Yellow Antwerp have always been esteemed sorts; the red are large and of fine flavour, and the yellow also large, yellow, sweet, and very good for dessert. The Sweet Yellow Antwerp has slender shoots, and is (Mr. Rivers says) the sweetest of all.

Rivers's Black is a hybrid (I believe crossed with the blackberry) very dark in colour, and with a certain acidity of flavour, which gives piquancy when it is mixed with the other kinds in jam.

The Fastolf or Filby Raspberry is red, large, and excellent; it has pretty well superseded the Antwerp, being quite as good in flavour, much larger, and an excellent bearer. It has, besides, the good quality of sometimes producing a crop of fine autumnal raspberries, superior to the fruit of the double-bearing kinds. The double-bearing is, in fact, an autumn raspberry.

Carter's Prolific is deep red in colour, large and good in flavour. Vice-President French is a large, round, deep red raspberry, which is very rich and good in flavour. Cutbush's Prince of Wales is fine in size, red, firm, and very good. Fillbasket is a large, good raspberry, and a most abundant bearer.

As good autumn-bearing kinds there are October Red and October Yellow, or Merveille des Quatre Saisons, and Merveille des Quatre Saisons Jaune; both are large, bear abundantly in autumn, with long spikes of fruit, and are excellent in flavour.

Large Orange is a handsome fruit, of peculiar flavour.

I believe the usual price of canes is from 1s. 6d. to 6s. per dozen. There are but few kinds as dear as the last price; excellent common sorts are 1s. 6d. and many *new* choice ones 3s. and 4s. Carter's Large Orange is, I believe, 1s. a root.

CHAPTER XXIX.

STRAWBERRIES.

Possibly the main thing which makes strawberries the especial favourites they are is their earliness. Unless we are lucky enough to possess the best-keeping sorts of apples and pears, they come upon us when home-ripened fruit has been for months unknown at our tables, and when the first warm weather renders their refreshing deliciousness doubly acceptable. In themselves, however, without this favourable introduction, they have quite merit enough to make them welcome, and the additional advantage of being plentiful and cheap, as well as choice and excellent. The earliest luxury of the season to the gardenless Londoner is his pottle of strawberries, bought for sixpence or so, whereas as good a dish of almost any other fruit would cost much more.

Although the strawberry is rather an uncertain crop, most owners of a garden can compass the growth of a small supply, and there is no fruit that better repays the grower, on account of its superior excellence when fresh gathered, to the finest the market can supply, if only a day old.

Strawberries like a good loamy soil of some depth. If the soil be loose and sandy, it must be made firmer and more stable with a mixture of marl or clay, and if it be too heavy, it should be rendered more open by mixing in sand, road-scrapings, very fine cinder-ash, or burnt or charred materials. Boggy or peaty land requires burning, or the application of good mould; and if it is wet, draining is necessary.

They are propagated by runners, which are thrown out by strings from the sides of the old roots, round which they take root. Those nearest the plant should be marked to save, as the best. When these runners have taken root, they may either remain where they are until autumn, or they may at once be taken up and planted in rows in the nursery, five or six inches apart. If they are taken up, and thus planted out, they will make fine, large, well-rooted plants, strong enough to bear fruit the next year.

New sorts are reared from seed which is cleared from the pulp, sown and kept safe from mice and accidents until the little plants grow.

For making new beds, trench the ground two spits, *i. e.*, twenty inches deep: the good soil should be as deep as this, and the trenching must not go below it: a good allowance of half-rotten manure may be mixed with the first spit. If the runners rooted in summer have been well taken care of, they may be finally planted any time before frost makes the ground hard to work. Beds may be made of four rows of strawberries each, with two or three feet between the beds. They also do very well made into a border, two or three rows deep, outside fruit trees, as far round the garden as the aspect is sufficiently sunny for them. Some prefer planting in single rows, or in groups of three or four. The strong growing kinds may be planted 15 inches apart every way, those of medium growth 15 inches between the rows, and 12 from plant to plant, and others respectively 12 or 9 inches, according to their luxuriance.

The first year cut all the runners from the plants before they take root, to throw strength into the parent. If they show for fruit, spread cut grass or straw between the roots, both to keep the fruit clean and to retain the moisture in the beds. As soon as the fruit is gathered rake this off, keep the ground clean with the hoe, and let the plants grow until winter. Then, *and not sooner,* cut off the leaves and fork the beds over carefully. The second summer the plants will bear a fine crop.

Established beds should be kept free from weeds by hoeing them up in dry weather, and the beds should be set in order late in spring, all useless strings and runners cleared away, with care not to injure the foliage, and sticks placed against sterile plants, as soon as known. When the bloom trusses show spread grass or straw under them, and from that time until the fruit begins to ripen, the plants should never suffer from drought. By the time the fruit is gathered plenty more runners will have grown. These should all be cleared away about the end of August, as they exhaust the soil, and the old roots too; but great care must be taken not to injure the leaves of the plants, as they have yet the important work to do of preparing for the next year's bloom. Pull up all the sterile plants, and fill their places with well-established runners. The next attention the strawberries require, except keeping under the weeds, is to cut away all the decayed and injured foliage in winter. If the rows are far apart, dig a small trench between them and fill it with decayed manure, and if the rows are too close together for this, give a good top-dressing.

A bank or mound, running from east to west, and with the slopes consequently facing north and south, is good for the production of early and late strawberries. The south slope may be planted with Black Prince and Keen's Seedling, and the north with Elton. The slopes should be at an angle of 45°. Sea-weed and sea-weed ash is a good manure for strawberries; liquid manure may be applied with advantage; and some recommend mulching, just as the plants are coming into flower. In light ground give liquid manure in the spring.

To obtain roots for forcing, place small pots filled with good, sound compost, and make the earliest runners that can be had root in them. When these small pots are full of root, remove the young plants into larger, place them in an open situation, and water them sufficiently. By the end of September they will have stout buds, and may be plunged for the winter; but forcing must begin very gently, and they must have a moist atmosphere. Commence with 55°, and by the time the leaf is developed, raise it to 60°. Keep the plants near the glass, give them plenty of air, and the less advance there is on the 60° of heat the better.

Alpine strawberries are grown to produce autumn fruit. They bear cooler, damper, more shady situations than most kinds, and will do in a lighter soil. The fruit is conical, it has a peculiar aromatic flavour, and it is fine for preserving whole. Some recommend growing them from seed, chosen from choice specimens, sown the end of January, in gentle heat. Prick out the seedlings in boxes, keep them under glass, harden them off in April, and plant them out finally on an elevated bed, in a sunny situation. They must be watered in dry weather, and when the fruit forms, it may have tiles or slates placed under it to save it from rotting in the autumn rains. Some in preference raise them from runners, like other kinds, selecting them from the finest, truest Alpine; the fruit should be large, broad at its base, and sharply conical. If the young plants are planted in August, do not clear the bed of runners the following summer, as with other kinds, as the runners rooted then will produce fruit in the autumn, and until quite late. Finer autumn fruit may be produced by cutting off all the flowers until the end of June, and the result will be a supply of fine fruit from the end of July until the frost. Alpines may be planted only six or eight inches apart; and it is a good plan to plant some, both red and white, on a north border, and to retard them further by removing them every year. There are several varieties: the White Alpine, small and white; Blanche d'Orleans, white also, but producing larger fruit; Brune de Gilbert, and Gallande, both small, very dark in colour, and abundant bearers; the Red Alpine, scarlet and productive. All bear in summer and autumn.

The red and white Wood strawberries are similar in character, but bear in summer only. The fruit is round, small, and pleasant in flavour. They are not often cultivated. They require the same management as the Alpine, except that the spring flowers are not cut down, but the fruit allowed to perfect itself as soon as it will.

The Black Prince is a very early strawberry, nice in flavour, and a most abundant bearer, if the locality suits it, not otherwise. The leaves are smooth, dark, and firm, with obtuse serrations. The fruit is of medium size, polished on the surface, and very dark-coloured.

Keen's Seedling is a good early strawberry, large, deep crimson, with a fine brisk flavour.

The Old Pine, or Carolina, will about follow these. It is a bright scarlet, large, rich, and excellent in flavour. Stirling Castle Pine is larger, and equal to it in excellence of flavour, and Carolina Superba is also a fine strawberry. Myatt's Pine is fine, but rare.

The British Queen is a splendid strawberry, as regards size, and it is pretty good in flavour.

The White Carolina is a sweet, nice, and exceedingly pretty strawberry, deserving more attention than it gets, and it is also a good bearer. It is such a beautiful strawberry in its delicately tinted whiteness, that a dish of it is a picture. Some complain of it as woolly, but let it only be gathered before it gets dead-ripe, and few will surpass it in flavour.

There is a variegated-foliaged Pine, which is very ornamental growing, but I believe the fruit has no great merit, and the plants are weakly, and poor bearers.

The characteristics of the Hautbois are tall growing, rough, pale green leaves of thin texture, tall stalks, middle-sized fruit, and a great propensity to produce sterile plants, which must be guarded against by rooting up all the unfertile plants as soon as they are detected. Rivers's Royal Hautbois is large, fine in flavour, and a most abundant bearer. Mr. Rivers writes, "The ground under my plants of this sort is always literally paved with large fruit of the most exquisite flavour."

Other good strawberries are numerous. Eleanor is large, late, and a good bearer; Eliza is a good bearer; Elton is a fine late strawberry, of a rich, deep colour, and fine, rather sharp flavour. Eleanor and Elton are especially good for preserving. Besides these, there are many new and first-class kinds, descriptions of which will be found in the catalogues which are sent out by most growers of high standing.

Alpines are the first to bring into bearing by forcing. The plants must be potted in March or April, and kept with the pots sunk in earth, in a shady spot, until there is danger of frost, when they must be placed under shelter. From November or so, they may be forced with gentle heat, and they will bear through the winter.

The Roseberry is a good sort to force to come in early in the year. Pot runners of the year in May or June; as bloom and runners show, nip them off, plunge the pots, and bring them into the forcing-house in January. Put them near the glass, give the pots pans, and water the plants when they need it, and only in the pans after the flowers come. As the fruit swells, pinch off some of the leaves, to give light and air. Pines may be got ready in the same manner, to be brought into the house in February and March. A sufficient number of all the good forcing sorts should be provided to bring in, a few at a time, in succession. The Roseberry has the merit of doing with less light than most kinds; and Keen's Seedling is excellent to follow it.

Roseberries, when they have done producing in the house, may be planted out in a bed of rich earth, and have the leaves cut off. Plants thus treated will produce a fine second crop in August and September, after which they will be of no further use. The Pines, after they have borne in the house, may be plunged, in their pots, in a shady border, and they will do for forcing a second year.

CHAPTER XXX.

MULBERRIES, MEDLARS, AND NUTS.

ANY ordinary garden soil will do for the mulberry, if it be not too clayey, but it prefers mellow, naturally rich earth, not that which is made rich with manure, unless the growth becomes sluggish from old age, when top-dressing with good compost will be useful.

It is usually propagated by cuttings or layers. The old plan of using for cuttings only the young shoots, as in currants, is discontinued, and truncheons of considerable size are now taken in preference, thus producing bearing young trees in a much shorter time. Cuttings of young shoots may be taken at the fall of the leaf. Plant them in the autumn, leaving only about two buds exposed.

Large truncheons may be cut in February: set them a foot deep in the earth, and roll moss round all the portion which is above ground, except the upper pair of buds. This is to prevent evaporation, and the situation chosen should be sheltered from direct sunshine and wind.

For layering, shoots of the year before are used. The layers may be laid down either in November or February; they may be slit or ringed, or they will root without; and the young plants may be divided from the parent tree at the end of one year. They should be planted in the nursery for two years, trained as standards during that period, and then they will be fit for their final destination. Common grafting seldom does well, but inarching will make strong young trees in a short time.

Seedlings may be reared as in the case of other berries.

A young tree for a standard should have a straight stem without blemishes, with no more than three or four regular shoots for a head. When the tree has been planted a year, and has taken to the soil, cut back these shoots to three or four inches, and they will each put out several shoots. In August choose four of the strongest and best placed, and cut out all the rest, that they may grow, and ripen the extremities. The following spring the head should be thinned out, leaving only the well-placed shoots. The mulberry bears both on short-jointed young wood and on spurs, not on gross shoots, which must be thinned out and stopped, and not allowed to crowd the growth of the tree.

For the winter pruning, take out cross shoots wherever they are crowded. The shady side of the tree may be kept thinner than the sunny side, and watery spray growing from the branches in the middle of the tree should be removed. No shortening is needed except in the case of over-rampant branches, which may be cut back, and their place supplied with fresh leaders.

Mulberries bear forcing, and the fruit may be ripened early in July. The trees may be planted in a bed in the house, or grown in pots for the purpose. They will bear a high temperature.

The Black mulberry is the kind cultivated for eating in England. The White is spoken of for feeding silkworms; but it is seldom seen. Young mulberry trees are bought for from 3s. 6d. to 5s. each, and larger for from £1 to £5. It is a touchy tree to remove. A good tree produces a great quantity of fruit, which should be eaten as gathered, to be in perfection.

Most owners of a garden like to have one medlar tree, or perhaps more, if there be plenty of room to spare. Blake's Large and Dutch produce large fruit; but the Nottingham bears fruit which is, although smaller in size, much better in flavour. The Stoneless is inferior; but the fruit keeps longer than any other kind. The Royal is a new sort from France, which is like the Nottingham in flavour, good in size, and an abundant bearer. Trees may be bought for 1s. 6d, or 2s. each.

The soil which suits the medlar best is a well-drained but retentive loam. The best modes of propagation are by layers or by grafting. Layers of shoots of the last year are laid down in February or March, and they will root by the autumn. Grafting is sometimes done on the white-thorn; but it seldom produces good trees, because the stock is of much slower growth than the scion. On the pear stock it thrives much better. It is best to train up the stock standard high, and then graft or bud it.

Standard medlars must be managed in forming their heads like standard plums. The shoots are less numerous; but they have a trick of turning in a wrong direction, likely to distort the head of the tree, so that they should often be looked over, to correct their vagrancy and to give the tree a good head.

The fruit should not be gathered until November, i.e., not before it is fully matured, or it shrivels, instead of ripens, as it softens. When dry, after gathering, they should be spread out singly, the calyx, or open side, downwards, on a bed of sand. If the stalk end is previously dipped in strong brine of salt and water, it is said to keep the medlars from getting mouldy.

Propagating medlars by seed is too tedious for most growers, as it generally lies two years in the ground before it grows. Those who wish to try it must let the fruit thoroughly decay, and then sow the seed in light soil, water the seedlings often when the weather is dry, and thin them to two feet apart. When the young trees are four or five years old, they will be fit for planting out.

Those who have plenty of ground may like to grow nuts, and will find them a satisfactory crop. By nuts we generally mean Filberts, and those of the same kind, the *Corylus avellana*. The chief kinds are the White and Red Filbert. They differ only in one having a pale, the other a reddish-brown skin. The Prolific Cob is a fine, large nut; and the Cosford is thin in the shell, good in flavour, and a great bearer. The Prolific Dwarf takes little room, and so is good for small gardens, as it is also a great bearer. Gordon's Thin-shelled is a good sort. The Frizzled is very ornamental, and like other nuts in other respects. The Purple Filbert is purple in leaves and fruit, and equal to the Red Filbert in size and flavour. The Kentish Cob, or Lambert's Filbert, is very late and very good, and the Merveille de Bolwyller is large, good in flavour, and a plentiful bearer. Nut trees may be bought for 6s. a dozen: these are generally about two or three feet high, and grown on their own roots. Mr. Rivers, of Sawbridgeworth, recommends the above-named kinds grafted on the Spanish Hazelnut; trees of this kind are 2s. 6d.

each; they are four feet high, and are recommended as emitting no suckers, and forming handsome and prolific garden trees.

Any pretty good ordinary soil will do for nuts provided it does not hold stagnant moisture, but a free upland, light loam suits them best, and a plentiful mixture of decayed leaf-mould is good for them.

They are more frequently increased by layers than by any other mode. Shoots of the previous year's growth may be laid down in autumn or in spring, before the buds open, and they will root readily. By the end of the year the young plants may be separated from the parent tree, and planted out a foot apart, in rows three feet apart. In planting them, prune them to only one shoot each, the best, and cut that back to a foot or eighteen inches, according to its strength. As they grow, keep them to a single stem of a foot and a half or two feet high, before the head forms, which makes it easy to keep the root free from suckers. As the head forms, it is quite worth while to train it to a good shape, keeping it thin and open, and cutting away irregular, superfluous, and rampant shoots.

Young trees may be made from cuttings, which should be taken about a foot and a half long, and all the buds, except a few nearest the top, should be picked out, to prevent the after-growth of suckers.

Nuts are often also grafted, using the common Hazel and Spanish Hazel as stocks. The time for it is, as with apples and pears, when the buds begin to swell.

Raising from seed is little resorted to, except for rearing common Hazels; but hybrydizing might be practised without difficulty in trees which, like the nut, bear the male and female flowers apart, so that crossing might be managed with ease.

For the winter pruning of nuts, thin out all the cross shoots and superfluous spray, and cut back rampant shoots to half their length, to induce them to throw out fruitful shoots for future produce. Nuts produce on shoots of the preceding year, which have been well exposed to the light to ripen them. The beginning of February is a good time for pruning, as by then the blossom shows itself; the female has a pretty little pink brush, and the male has the well-known catkin, as much as compatible with due thinning out, avoid cutting away the bloom, especially the female. Filberts will often have a good show of female blossom, and scarcely any catkins: in this case there will be no fruit unless catkins can be brought at the time the farina is about to shed, and branches with them tied to the trees amongst the flowers. Catkins from wild nuts will do.

After the winter pruning, nut trees require little except the removal of the suckers, and letting light into the centres, by cutting out ill-placed, watery growth. Those intended for dwarf growth should be watched, kept within bounds, and trained to a compact, good shape.

Nuts, to keep well, should be thoroughly ripe before they are gathered, and well dried before they are stored. After they are gathered, lay them in heaps, or put them in hampers, let them sweat for a week, and then expose them to sun and air for another week. After this they may be simply packed in stone jars, left open for a fortnight, examined to see if they sweat again, allowed to get perfectly dry in the jars, and then covered down. Any damp about them will turn them musty, and spoil them entirely, so of course they must be stored in a cool, dry place. To impart a fresh-looking colour to the husks, some persons sulphur them, placing them in a close vessel, with a pan of sulphur smouldered under them; but they eat better without this treatment. Lambert's Filbert is the best kind for keeping a very long time, and next to that comes the Frizzled Cob.

Walnut trees may be purchased for 1s. 6d. each, and those who have plenty of room to spare, and years of possession of land before them, will be repaid for planting. They thrive in a deep, loamy soil. The large French Walnut, Noyer à Bijou, is handsome, and good in flavour. The Noyer de St. Jean has the advantage in our climate of blossoming after the spring frosts; but the Dwarf Prolific Walnut, *Juglans præpar-*

turiens, Noyer Fertile of the French, deserves the especial attention of growers. The young trees will sometimes bear when only two feet high; different specimens vary in fertility, but any walnut which bears so early must be worth growing.

CHAPTER XXXI.

FIGS.

Figs can only be grown with success in a warm situation, for hot, glowing sunshine is more to them than soil. There are few parts of England, except the far West, and the genial Channel Islands, where they bear abundantly, but in warm, sheltered spots on the warm chalk of Kent, and in similar situations, they will, in fine seasons, produce plentiful crops of well-flavoured fruit.

A warm, genial summer is what they require: if there be over-much wet they crack before they ripen.

A chalky loam is said to be the soil which suits the fig best, but almost any good, rather light garden soil will do for it. The ground must not be much manured, as that will encourage a too rampant growth.

The fig roots firmly from cuttings. Take the cuttings of ripe wood, about four inches long, plant them in pots in January or February, plunge the pots in a moderate hotbed, and by the end of summer you will have nice little plants, fit for either fruiting in pots or for planting out. If the young plants are wanted for forcing, pot them when rooted, bring them forward with bottom heat, and treat them much the same as vines. Those which are to go into the open ground should be planted out when there is no longer danger of frost. If the roots have become crowded in the pots, spread them nicely in planting them.

The fig propagates freely by layers, and also by suckers taken from the parent tree, and shaded and sheltered until they take to growing.

In England, fig trees require protection in winter, covering them up with mats, straw, fern, spruce, or boughs, before the time of severe frost, and removing the mats as soon as it seems over: fern or straw may remain a little longer, and spruce until the time for pruning. The pruning must not be done until the buds begin to swell.

Old, useless boughs may be cut out entirely. In the growing period remove superfluous shoots, when the young shoots are about three inches long, leaving those which are short and compact growing. If the tree is trained, reserve what are wanted for covering blank spots. All the useless spray must be removed until about August, as growth of the sort will often continue until then, especially in moist summers. By this means all the wood for bearing next year will get good exposure to sun and air. When the little figs are the size of nutmegs, the ends of the shoots may be nipped off to encourage their swelling, and all suckers must be destroyed from time to time when necessary.

Where a wall is required for the fig, as it is in most localities, horizontal training is best, and ample space is required for it. It is said figs may be grown as bushes in gardens as far north as London, and in parts of England south of that, if they are taken up early in November, without disturbing the earth round the roots, kept in a cellar until there is no longer danger of spring frosts, and then planted out where they were taken from. Figs thus treated will ripen a crop of fruit in September.

Young fig trees may be bought for 2s. 6d. and 3s. 6d. each, and of larger size for 5s.

The kinds are numerous.

The White Marseilles, the Madeleine of France, White Naples, or White Standard, is a fig of luscious sweetness, which bears abundantly, and does well for forcing. The fruit is of medium size, roundish, ribbed, yellowish-green when fully ripe, and ripening in August. It will ripen in England against a wall, and in a warm locality it does as a standard. Mr. Rivers states that this will thrive and bear two crops in the year in an orchard-house with boarded floor, without heat.

The Brown Turkey, or Lee's Perpetual, has also many other names. The fruit is large, pear-shaped, and brownish-red, covered with blue bloom. The flesh is red and luscious in flavour, the tree is hardy, grows to a full size, and is one of the best for growing as a standard out of doors. It ripens in August and September. It bears most abundantly in pots and on walls, and is a good kind for forcing. The Dwarf Prolific is similar to the Brown Turkey, and a great bearer, but of a dwarf habit of growth.

The Early Violet is a small, roundish fig, brown-red, with a bloom over the skin, red in flesh and good in flavour, ripening in August. The tree is hardy and a good bearer. It does well for pot-culture and for forcing. Mr. Rivers states that in the forcing-house it will give three crops in one year.

The Black Ischia is a medium-sized, very dark fig, deep red inside, sweet and rich in flavour, hardy, and a good bearer. The fruit ripens in August, and the trees do well in pots. The figs are roundish, flattened at the top. The Brown Ischia is lighter in colour, very good, early, hardy, and bears as a standard in favourable situations. Against a wall it will bear two crops.

The Brunswick is large, pear-shaped, oblique at the end, green on the shady side, brown on the sunny, pink in the centre, white near the skin, semi-transparent, rich, sweet, and high-flavoured; it ripens in August, and is one of the most useful of the hardy figs, being hardy and an excellent bearer, the best of any for out-door cultivation against a wall, but not good for forcing.

The Angélique (Madeleine according to some) is small, pyramidal, yellow, dotted with green-white specks, white in the interior, but reddish round the seeds, and not very rich in flavour, but very good, with an agreeable perfume. Unless under very favourable circumstances, it will not ripen without artificial heat, but it forces well, and bears abundantly.

Adam is a new variety from France. The fruit is the largest of any, roundish, brown-purple, and very handsome. The tree has a fine, bold foliage, and is rather apt to cast the fruit before it ripens.

The Large White Genoa is a fine fig of excellent flavour, white outside, red in the flesh, and ripe the end of August, but it is a poor bearer.

The Malta, or Small Brown, is small, pale brown throughout when fully ripe, compressed at the stalk, and becoming ripe by the end of August. It is very sweet and nice in flavour, and if it remain on the tree until it shrivels, it is quite like a sweetmeat.

Pregussata is small, round, compressed at both ends, purplish-brown, with pale spots on the sunny side, deep red inside, and very rich and luscious. It is an excellent fig, in use from August to October, and very good for forcing.

The White or Green Ischia is a very pretty-looking fig, the white skin being so transparent as to show the purple flesh through it, when fully ripe. It ripens the end of August, and is rich and delicious in flavour. The tree has a small habit of growth, and is a great bearer. It is well adapted to pot-culture, and forcing.

The Black and Brown Ischia, and Brown Turkey, are the best to grow as standards, and they and most of the other kinds named above do well against a wall. They, the White Ischia, Angélique, Early Violet, Marseilles, and Pregussata, are good for pot-culture and for forcing. Figs should be eaten almost as soon as they are gathered.

CHAPTER XXXII.

VINES.

It would be out of place in a little work especially devoted to the fruit garden, to enter elaborately into the cultivation of the grape-vine in green-houses and hothouses; but its treatment out of doors, on walls or roofs, succeeds sufficiently when the culture is judicious, the kind appropriate, and the summer warm and favourable, to deserve a short chapter.

The vine, to give it a fair chance of producing sweet, eatable fruit, must have a mellow, well-drained soil. An ordinary sandy loam is the best foundation, but if the bed be of any common garden soil, it should be one which will imbibe and transmit moisture easily. Vine roots will go down very deep, but it is not desirable to let them: it is, therefore, well to plant on stations. (*See* STATIONS.) First see that the ground is sufficiently drained, and then lay the foundation, or make the station of some imperishable material—stone, brick, or clinkers, rammed tight together. About eighteen inches of earth above this will suffice. The soil must afterwards be looked to and corrected as it may require. If if wants richness, mix in fresh manure and plenty of decayed leaves. Any decayed vegetable matter is good, and a portion of it should be of an enduring character, which will give out its enriching qualities slowly and lastingly. Coarse bone-manure, nubbly charcoal, burnt wood, and brushwood are good. If the situation is cold and damp, the bed may be raised several inches above the path.

Vines are now generally propagated from eyes or buds. Pieces are saved after the autumn pruning, cut into lengths, and imbedded in moist soil until winter. Choose a nice eye, cut the wood off half an inch above the eye, in a sloping direction from the eye, and cut it off horizontally one inch below the eye. Insert each bud in a five-inch pot, take care that no worms can get in, and plunge the pots in bottom heat of from 70° to 80°. When the young plants are something like a foot high, they should be shifted into seven-inch pots, well drained, and filled in with rich, turfy soil. Some gardeners reserve a bit of the two years' old wood at the base of each eye.

Raising young vines from layers used formerly to be more practised than it is now. Young wood may be put down any time between November and March, and no tongue or slit need be made in it. Before vines were raised from buds so much, nurserymen used often to keep old vines in pots for the purpose of making young plants. The shoots were layered round them in pots about February, and would be saleable plants by the autumn. If it be preferred, a growing shoot, with a portion of the previous year's wood, may be layered.

Vines may be raised from cuttings, which should be taken while in a state of rest. If they have two eyes each, it will suffice, and they should be cut on a slant, just below the lower bud. Plant them singly in small pots of good mould, with the top bud just below the surface. Give bottom heat, and shift the young plants into larger pots as they require it, *i. e.*, as those in use fill with root. In the spring, place them in the stove, if there be one at command, and remove them from there to the green-house, allowing them plenty of air, to prevent their running up weak.

Speechly recommends using for cuttings two inches of two years' old wood, and one bud or eye of the new, planted in pots with the bud just level with the surface of the mould. Thick shoots of three or four years' old wood, of greater length, will root. They may be put in at once against a wall, or they should be planted in very deep pots, as nearly the whole length must be buried. In all cases bottom heat facilitates rooting.

Vines raised from cuttings or eyes should be kept under glass for their first year, and they will benefit much from a judicious allowance of liquid manure during the summer months.

Inarching is the kind of grafting most practised on vines. Common grafting is very seldom used. When it is, the stock should be forward; it may even have unfolded some of its leaves. Whip-grafting is best; the graft should have two eyes, and it is a good plan to cover the whole, even the buds of the scion, with moss, and to keep the moss damp.

Vines for out-of-doors culture may be planted out the end of March. If they are from pots, shake the earth gently from the roots, uncoil them, spread them out in a fan shape, spread a little good compost over them, and cover the surface with three inches of coarse charred material, which will absorb heat and admit water when wanted. The young vines will only require training until the autumn, when they must be cut back to three or four eyes. The next year the shoots from these eyes must be trained to any required form. They should not be at all crowded.

When a young vine of one shoot is cut back to three or four eyes, each eye will of course become a shoot. As soon as they are long enough to nail to the wall, the two best must be chosen, and trained horizontally, about a foot from the ground. When these are two feet and a half long, the ends may be turned upwards and trained perpendicularly for two or three feet, according to their strength, and then stopped, by nipping off the ends; laterals produced after that time should also be stopped. When the shoots from the two horizontal branches are long enough to require nailing in, three on each must be selected; one near the end, one a foot nearer the main stem, and a third between that and the main stem: these should be nailed in perpendicular lines, allowed to grow until they are about four feet long, and then stopped.

If young vines are not strong when first put in, they had better be cut back to two eyes: select the best shoot, train it up, and then proceed as above.

To take up the progress of the trained vines: in the next autumn pruning, cut down every alternate shoot to two eyes, and leave the others for fruit, two or three feet long, according to their strength. It must always be remembered that vines produce on young wood of the present year, grown from eyes of one-year-old wood.

If each shoot produces more than half a dozen bunches of grapes, the bunches should be reduced to that number. Each shoot which is cut back will produce two shoots from the two eyes left; the best must be chosen, and trained upright to produce the next year, and those which have produced must be cut back to two eyes.

On a *very* high wall, a second series may find room. Top-dressing and manuring are good for the vine, and care must be taken that the roots are not interfered with by digging too near to them. As general summer culture, all superfluous spray must be removed, and the bearing shoots stopped an eye or two beyond the fruit. This thinning is valuable in letting in sun and air.

To get fine grapes, one bunch to a square foot of wall will be enough to leave. The grapes in the bunches, too, must be thinned out, first when they are the size of peas, and again when they are the size of gooseberries. Scissors are used for the purpose, and the grapes in the interior of the bunch are cut away, sparing those which grow outwards. After the last thinning, every grape should stand quite apart from its neighbours. It is a tedious job, but the fruit will not turn out good for much without it; and in a season which is sufficiently favourable to ripen grapes out of doors, *i. e.*, one of tolerable forwardness and heat, the fruit will prove deserving attention and trouble, which will add to its flavour and colour as well as to its size. The lateral shoots, too, should be stopped and never allowed to too much shade or crowd the fine foliage. In September the stopped laterals may be cut away, to give circulation of air, and to let the heat of the sun get to the wall. Then, too, the grapes must be protected from flies and wasps.

The best kind of all for a wall, or the outside of a house, is the Esperione, which is extraordinarily prolific, very hardy, and of luxuriant growth. It perfects its fruit well, is a very superior grape, and even in unfavourable seasons does better than any other sort. The bunches are handsomely shouldered, and the grapes differ little in size from Black Hamburghs grown under glass; they are large, round, inclining to oblate, very dark purple, with a blue bloom, rather firm, sweet, juicy, and good in flavour. The grapes ripen better and earlier out of doors than the Black Hamburgh. The leaves are variously cut, and they dye to a yellow colour, not red.

The Chasselas de Fontainebleau is a good out-of-doors white grape. The bunches are long, loose-shouldered, sometimes compact and cylindrical, the grapes large, and generally round, firm, juicy, and sweet. It is hardy and productive, and ripens its grapes with certainty. Against a south wall it ripens in September, and in a favourable season the bunches will hang on the vine until November. The leaves are middle-sized, roundish, with an open base, slightly and regularly lobed, smooth on both sides, pale green, and becoming yellow late in the autumn.

The August Muscat, or Muscat d'Août, is a deep purple grape, rich and juicy, with a slight Muscat flavour, ripening on a wall out of doors, about the end of August. The grapes are of medium size, inclining to oval, and the vine has a dwarf habit of growth, which fits it very well for pot-culture. It is rather delicate.

The Sweetwater is the best-known, and most generally grown, of all out-of-doors grapes. The bunches grow very thick and clustering, and if the weather be at all unfavourable when the vine is in flower, they are badly formed, with numerous very small fruit crowded in them. The bunches are middle-sized, and the grapes are very juicy and sweet, but not high-flavoured. It ripens well on a south wall in dry, warm seasons. The wood is short-jointed.

The Black Hamburgh ripens against a wall, in a favourable situation. The bunches are large, broad-shouldered, conical, and well set; the grapes rather oval, deep blue black, with a rich bloom, very juicy, sweet, and full-flavoured. The vine is a good bearer, and the bunches are regularly formed and handsome, and will hang long. In autumn the foliage fades off to green and yellow. It is a good sort for all purposes.

The Black Prince is another dark grape, which will

ripen its fruit out of doors under favourable circumstances. The bunches are rather long, and the grapes of a good size, when well thinned out. The flesh is white, sweet, juicy, and nice-flavoured; and when the grape is pulled from the stalk, a red receptacle, covered with the white flesh, is left. The seeds are numerous and large, the leaves are broad, thick, long in the stalk, tinged with red, not deeply cleft, broadly serrated, and changing in autumn to pale red and purple. The vine is a great bearer, and the grapes colour well.

The Black Cluster is quite one of the best out-of-doors grapes we have,—so good that it has been stated that it might be grown with us out of doors for wine. It is the real Burgundy. In Burgundy it is highly esteemed for wine; it is extensively grown for that purpose on the Rhine and Moselle, and is much used for champagne. The bunches are small, cylindrical, and compact; the grapes round, or a little oval, thin in the skin, blue-black, covered with bloom, juicy, sweet, and rich in flavour. It ripens well against a wall in the open air. This is better than Miller's Burgundy (which has downy leaves), the grapes of which are also not so large.

The Pitmaston White Cluster is rather larger than the Black Cluster, compact in the bunch, and shouldered; it ripens on a south wall earlier than the Sweetwater; the fruit is round, a little flattened at the top, amber-coloured when ripe, rather bronzed, with russet next the sun, and pleasant in flavour.

Among these, perhaps the best kinds to select are the Esperione, Black Cluster, Chasselas, Black Hamburgh, Black Prince, and Sweetwater, on walls which are pretty well placed; and in less favourable localities try the White Cluster, or White Chasselas.

CHAPTER XXXIII.

MELONS.

Melons in pits belong rather to the green-house and forcing department than to the fruit garden, but kitchen-gardens may accommodate a hotbed, on which a moderate supply may be produced, and turn out very well.

Melons do best with a bottom heat of about 80°, and atmospheric heat averaging about 75°. As sunlight increases, they will bear an increase, both to roots and branches, of from 5° to 10°. To make the hotbed, throw the fresh manure in a heap, and let it lie for a week. There should be a good mass of it; fifteen loads for each light will not be found too much, and by the end of a week it will have become very hot. Turn it over, shaking out every lock or patch, and when it has lain for about four days longer, water it well. Let it lie a few days more, turn it over again, and water the dry places. In another week it will be fit for use, but another turning will do good. It must be on a dry or well-drained spot, exposed to the full day's sun, and sheltered sideways from winds which would lower the temperature. If the ground below be on a slope, so that the manure is equal in thickness all over the bed, so much the better. Make a hollow in the centre of each light, half as deep as the bed, place brickbats at the bottom, over them some half-rotten manure, over that a flat square of turf upside down, and then the mould. Avoid planting out the young melon plants until there is no longer any danger of burning heat in the bed; and as the heat declines, keep it up with coatings of hot fermenting manure all round the bed, and as high as it. If the foundation of the bed be sunk, the coating (called by gardeners lining) must be sunk also to an equal depth. Place the frames on the bed, and test the heat of the bed and of the air inside.

Old seed is better than new, because the plants from it run less to leaf, and so give their strength more to the production of fruit. Give them bottom heat of from

75° to 85°. Before the second leaves come, the seedlings may be potted in five-inch pots, filled with strong loam, enriched with manure, two plants in each pot, and plunged in a temperature of from 70° to 80°. When a shoot sprouts from between the seed-leaves, nip it off, which will encourage two more fruitful shoots to sprout, and these will be enough for leaders. About a fortnight later they may be planted out in the bed.

As the melons progress, be it remembered, the bottom heat must never fall below 70°, nor rise above 90°, while the atmosphere in which they grow must not fall below 65°, nor rise above 80°, in general; but when the sun is out hot, it will be eight or ten degrees higher. Shade is fatal to the melon.

The seed may be sown about the middle of January. If, when the young plants are planted out, they have more than two shoots each, reduce them to that number. Water them when dry, according to the weather, watering also the sides of the frame, and the uncovered dung, once a day, or thereabouts. When fresh coatings are given, the insides of the frames against them must be well watered two or three times a week, to prevent burning.

When the plants begin to spread, introduce more earth, allowing from two to three barrowfuls to each light, from first to last. The bed should be raised in the middle, two plants set in the centre of each light, and a shoot led towards each corner.

When the shoots are within half a foot of the frame, stop them, by nipping off the ends, by that means encouraging lateral shoots to put out, and these will produce bloom of both kinds, generally more male than female flowers. Every day, in the middle of the day, because then the farina will be dry, the female bloom must be set. As soon as there are four fruit on each plant, swelled to about an inch long, or rather more, cut away all the flowers that show themselves, stop each shoot with fruit three or four eyes beyond it, and cut away all coarse growth which is likely to weaken the bearing parts. Connected with these, let there be good, healthy foliage, well exposed to the light; but let no inferior, late-formed leaves interfere with the older and finer ones.

Ventilation must be given every day, and the warmth from the external coatings must be kept up sufficiently to allow for the fall of temperature that it will occasion. Continue to water the sides of the frame occasionally, and when the melons are as large as hen's eggs, give liquid manure liberally; but always take care not to wet the collars of the plants. A week or two before the fruit begins to ripen, withhold water, and give extra ventilation.

None should attempt to grow melons who have not abundance of manure at command, as the quickest-growing require twelve or fourteen weeks to come to perfection, and some of the large sorts much longer. For small melons, the bed should be four feet deep, for larger ones, five feet, after they have settled; and they should be large as well as thick. A mixture of oak or chestnut leaves is good in giving lasting heat. The mould used must be rich and good. The over-head watering, which suits cucumbers, &c., so well, does not do with melons, which are only watered at the roots. The great difficulty in their culture is to unite plentiful ventilation and high temperature, both of which they require.

INDEX.

Acari, 49.
Acton Scot Peach, 117.
Alfriston apple, 93.
Almonds, 105.
—, varieties of, 106.
Alpine strawberries, 163.
American blight, 7, 46.
Annular budding, 24.
Aphides, 48.
Apparatus for protecting, 39.
Apple, or sweet quince, 83.
Apple, Alfriston, 93.
—, Beauty of Kent, 94.
—, Blenheim Orange, 97.
—, Calville Blanche, 100.
—, Codlins, 92.
—, Court of Wick, 101.
—, Downton Pippin, 95.
—, Emperor Alexander, 93.
—, Golden Noble, 99.
—, Golden Pippin, 94.
—, Golden Reinette, 102.
—, Golden Russet, 97.
—, Hawthornden, 93.
—, Irish Peach, 90.
—, Juneating, 90.
—, King of the Pippins, 96.
—, Lemon Pippin, 98.
—, Lord Suffield, 92.
—, Nonesuch, 94.
—, Norfolk Beaufin, 99.
—, Old Nonpareil, 100.
—, Red Quarenden, 91.
—, Ribston Pippin, 101.
—, Reinette de Canada, 98.
—, Reinette Anana, 97.
—, Scarlet Crofton, 94.
—, Scarlet Pearmain, 96.
—, Spring Grove Codlin, 92.
—, Summer Golden Pippin, 91.
—, Summer Pearmain, 96.
—, Wellington, 99.
—, White Astrakan, 91.
—, White Quarenden, 91.
—, Winter Nonesuch, 94.
Apples, 6, 27, 38, 86.
—, Autumn, 93.
—, bark beetle, 47.
—, as pyramids, 88.

Apples, cooking, 92, 99.
—, cordon horizontal training, 89.
—, early, 90.
—, eating, 90, 93, 100.
— for cider, 104.
— for cooking or eating, 97, 98.
—, on Crabs, 90.
—, planting, 88.
—, Rivers's list of, 103.
—, selection of, 102.
—, soil for, 86, 87.
—, stocks, 87.
—, weevil, 54.
Apricot moth, 51.
—, plum, 131.
—, Breda, 110.
—, Blenheim, 110.
—, Early Précoce, 109.
—, Hemskirke, 110.
—, Masculine, 109.
—, Moor Park, 109, 110.
—, Royal, 110.
Apricots, 106.
—, aspect for, 107.
—, pruning, 108.
—, soil for, 107.
—, training, 107, 108.
—, seedling, 107.
—, varieties, 109 to 111.
Autumn apples, 93.
—, pears, 70.
Averruncators, 56.

Baking pears, 83.
Baloon training, 32.
Bank for strawberries, 162.
Barrington peach, 118.
Beauty of Kent apple, 94.
Belle Agathe cherry, 144.
Belle de Jersey baking pear, 84.
Bellegarde peach, 118.
Bellisime d'Hiver baking pear, 84.
Beurré Clairgeau pear, 74.
— d'Amaulis pear, 67.
— de Capiaumont, 69.
— d'Aremberg, 76.
— Diel, 76.
— Rance, 78.

Bigarreau cherry, 142.
Birds, 41.
Bishop's Thumb pear, 63.
Black currants, 149.
— pear of Worcester, baking pear, 84.
— Eagle cherry, 141.
— Heart cherry, 140.
Blenheim apricot, 110.
— Orange apple, 97.
Blue Perdrigon plum, 129.
Breda apricot, 110.
Brignole prune, 132.
Bowed cuttings, 14.
Budding, 21 to 24.
— Peaches, 113.
Büttner's October cherry 145.

Cherry, Belle Agathe, 144.
—, Bigareau, 142.
—, Black Heart, 140.
—, Black Eagle, 141.
—, Büttner's October, 145.
—, Carnation, 142.
—, Downton, 141.
—, Early, 139.
—, Elton, 141.
—, Florence, 143.
—, Harrison's Heart, 141.
—, Kentish, 142.
—, Knight's Early Black, 140.
—, Late Duke, 140.
—, May Duke, 140.
—, Monstreuse de Jodoigne, 141.
—, Morello, 144.
—, Royal Duke, 141.
—, Small black, 143.
—, Tartarian black, 139.
—, Werder's Early Black Heart, 139.
—, White Heart, 143.
Cherries, 136.
—, pruning, 137.
Calebasse pear, 68.
Callus, 14.
Calville Blanche apple, 100.
Canker, 7, 42.
Caterpillars, 50.
Catillac baking pear, 85.

INDEX.

Carnation cherry, 142.
Chaumontelle pear, 76.
— for baking, 85.
Chancellor peach, 119.
Chermes, 50.
Cherry plum, 129.
Chinese quince, 83.
Chink grafting, 20.
Choosing trees, 6.
Cleft grafting, 19.
Coccus, 47.
Codlin moth, 53.
— stock, 87.
Codlins, 92.
Coe's Golden Drop plum, 133.
— Late Red, 134.
Convenience of dwarf trees, 36.
Cordon training, 36.
— horizontal training, 89.
Court of Wick apple, 101.
Crab stocks, 11.
Crassane pear, 73.
Cross fertilization, 13.
Crown grafting, 19.
Currants, 145.
—, prize, 156.
—, enemies to, 155.
—, on a single stem, 149.
Cuttings, 13, 14, 145.
— of gooseberries and currants, 149.

Damsons, 132.
Dexterity in budding, 23, 24.
Diagonal cordon training, 35.
Double grafting, 86.
Double-blossomed pear, 84.
Doucin stock, 11, 38.
Downton cherry, 141.
— Impératrice plum, 134.
— nectarine, 122.
— Pippin, 95.
Doyenné Blanc pear, 71.
Duc du Tellier nectarine, 123.
Duchesse d'Angoulême pear, 70.
Dwarf Prolific walnut, 171.

Early Admirable peach, 117.
— Anne peach, 116.
— apples, 90.
— Favourite plum, 128.
— May cherry, 139.
— Newington nectarine, 124.
— Orleans plum, 130.
— Prolific plum, 128.

Early Précoce apricot, 109.
— pears, 65, 67.
— York peach, 116.
Earwigs, 52.
Easter Beurré pear, 77.
Elruge nectarine, 123.
Elton cherry, 141.
Emperor Alexander apple, 93.
English paradise stock, 11.
Ermine moth, 51.
Espaliers, 31, 62.
Eyes, 14.

Fencing, 4.
Figs, 171.
—, cuttings of, 171.
—, soil for, 171.
—, varieties of, 172-174.
Figure of 8 moth, 52.
Florence cherry, 143.
Forcing strawberries, 162.
Forked sticks for gooseberries, 147.
Frame for fruit, 57.
Free stock, 11.
French paradise stock, 11.
Frigi domo, 39.
Fruit-buds and leaf-buds, 62.
Fruit-room, 56.

Gathering fruit, 59.
— medlars, 168.
German prune, 132.
Glout Morceau, 76.
Gnorimus nobilis, 46.
Goat moth, 46.
Golden Noble apple, 99.
— Pippin, 94.
— Reinette apple, 102.
— Russet apple, 97.
Gooseberry caterpillar, 51.
Gooseberries, 145.
—, on a single stem, 149.
—, prize, 147.
—, varieties of, 150 to 154.
Graciali pear, 67.
Grafts, 11.
Grafting, 12, 16 to 21.
— apples, 87.
— clay, 17.
— wax, 17.
Green chisel pear, 66.
Greengage plum, 128.
Grosse Mignonne peach, 117.
Gum, 45.

Hardwick nectarine, 122.
Harrison's Heart cherry, 141.
Hawthornden apple, 93.

Heat for melons, 181, 182.
Hedges, 5.
Hemskirke apricot, 110.
Hotbed for melons, 181.
Hot walls, 4.
Hunt's Tawny nectarine, 122.

In-arching, 20, 178.
Insects, 45 to 54.
Irish Peach apple, 90.
Iron hurdles for training, 31.

Jargonelle pears, 65.
Jaune Hâtive plum, 128.
Jefferson plum, 132.
Josephine de Malines pear, 78.
Juneating apple, 90.
— stock, 87.

Keeping apples, 97.
— cherries, 138.
Kentish cherries, 142.
King of the Pippins, 96.
Kirke's plum, 130.
Knight's Early Black cherry, 140.

Lackey moth, 54.
Ladybirds, 54.
Lancashire prize gooseberries, 154.
Late Admirable peach, 117.
— Duke cherry, 140.
Layering, 15.
Layers, 13.
Leaf destroyers, 47 to 54.
Lemon Pippin, 98.
Louise Bonne pear, 69.

Madeleine pear, or Citron des Calmes, 67.
Magnum Bonum plum, 13.
Magpie moth, 50.
Mahaleb stock, 12.
Manuring, 3, 10, 24, 25, 43, 109.
Masculine apricot, 109.
Marie Louise pear, 69.
Material for protection, 38.
May Duke cherry, 140.
Mealy bug, 47.
Medlars, 167.
Mellowing pears, 64.
Melon bed, 181.
— culture, 182, 183.
— seed, 182.
— varieties, 183.
Melons, 181.
—, heat for, 181.
Merry cherry, 143.

INDEX.

Mildew, 44.
Miller's list of pears, 80.
Monstreuse de Jodoigne cherry, 141.
Moor Park apricot, 109, 110.
Morello cherry, 144.
Mulberry, 165.
Murrey nectarine, 122.
Muscativerd pear, 66.

Napoleon pear, 70.
Nectarine, Downton, 122.
—, Duc du Tellier, 123.
—, Early Newington, 124.
—, Elruge, 123.
—, Hardwick, 122.
—, Hunt's Tawny, 122.
—, Murrey, 122.
—, New White, 124.
—, Old Newington, 125.
—, Peterborough, 125.
—, Pitmaston, 123.
—, Roman, 125.
—, Violette Hâtive, 123.
—, various, 125.
Nectarines, 122.
Netting trees, 42.
New White Nectarine, 124.
Niche-budding, 24.
Noblesse peach, 119.
Nonesuch apple, 94.
Norfolk Beaufin apple, 99.
Nursery, 5.
Nuts, 168.
—, seedling, 169.
—, to keep, 170.
—, varieties, 168.

Oidium, 44.
Old trees, 5, 29, 42, 43, 127.
— English codlin, 92.
— gardens, 28.
— Nonpareil apple, 100.
— Newington nectarine, 125.
Orange scale, 48.
Orchard, 1.
Orleans plum, 130.

Packing fruit, 59.
Paradise stocks, 11, 88.
Passe Colmar, 75.
Peaches, 111.
Peach border, 112.
—, budding, 113.
—, classes of, 116.
—, pruning, 114.
—, stone stocks, 113.
—, training, 114.
—, Acton Scot, 117.
—, Barrington, 118.
—, Bellegarde, 118.
— Chancellor, 119.

Peach, Early Anne, 116.
—, Early Admirable, 117.
—, Early York, 116.
—, Grosse Mignonne, 117.
—, Late Admirable, 117.
—, Noblesse, 119.
—, Red Nutmeg, 121.
—, Royal George, 118.
—, Salway, 121.
—, Smith's Newington, 119.
—, various, 121.
—, Walberton, 121.
Pear Blister moth, 51.
Pear-Quince, 83.
Pear, Beurré Clairgeau, 74.
—, Beurré d'Amaulis, 67.
—, Beurré d'Aremberg, 75.
—, Beurré de Capiaumont 69.
—, Beuvré Diel, 76.
—, Beurré Rance, 78.
—, Bishop's Thumb, 68.
—, Brown Beurré, 68.
—, Calebasse, 68.
—, Cassolette, Lechefrion, or Muscatverd, 66.
—, Citron de Calmes, 67.
—, Crassane, 73.
—, Chaumontelle, 76.
—, Doyenné Blanc, 71.
—, Duchesse d'Angoulême, 70.
—, Easter Beurré, 77.
—, Graciali, 67.
—, Glout Morceau, 76.
—, Green Chisel, 66.
—, Jargonelle, 65.
—, Josephine de Malines, 78.
—, Louise Bonne, 69.
—, Madeleine, 67.
—, Marie Louise, 69.
—, Napoleon, 70.
—, Passe Colmar, 75.
—, Seckle, 68.
—, Summer Bergamot, 66.
—, Swan's Egg, 67.
—, variegated Crassane, 74, 66.
—, William's Bon Chrétien, 66.
—, Windsor, 66.
—, Winter Nelis, 74
—, Zéphirine Grégoire, 73.
Pears, 27, 60 to 86.
—, gathering, 64, 65, 71, 72.
—, grafting, 60.
— on pear stocks, 35.
—, propagation of, 60, 61.
—, seedling, 61.
—, spurs, 63.
—, thinning, 63.
Peterborough nectarine, 125

Pine-apple scale, 48.
Pitmaston Orange Nectarine, 123.
Planting, 8.
Plum, Acari, 49.
Plum pruning, 127.
—, of good sorts, 135.
—, training, 126.
— stocks, 126.
Plums, 126.
—, apricot, 131.
—, Blue Perdrigon, 129.
—, Brignole Prune, 132.
—, Cherry, 129.
—, Coe's Golden Drop, 133.
—, Late Red, 134.
—, Damson, 132.
—, Downton Impératrice 134.
—, Early Favourite, 128.
—, Early Prolific, 128.
—, Early Orleans, 130.
—, German Prune, 132.
—, Greengage, 128.
—, Jaune Hâtive, 128.
—, Jefferson, 132.
—, Kirke's, 130.
—, Magnum Bonum, 135.
—, Orleans, 130.
—, Précoce de Tours, 127.
—, Saint Catherine, 134.
—, Violet Diaper, 132.
—, Violet Hâtive, 128.
—, Washington, 131.
—, Winesour, 133.
Portugal quince, 83.
Protection, 37 to 42, 109.
Protecting dwarf trees, 39, 42.
Pruning, 26 to 29, 34.
— peaches, 114.
Psylla, 50.
Purchasing trees, 6.
Pyramidal training, 32.
Pyramids, apple, 88.
— of apples on crabs, and pears on pear stocks, 89.

Quenouille training, 32.
Quinces, 82, 83.
Quince stocks, 12, 82.

Raspberries, 156.
—, cultivation of, 158, 159.
—, planting of, 157.
—, price of canes, 160.
—, seedling, 157.
—, varieties of, 159, 160.
Receipt of baking pears and quinces, 85.
Red currants, 154, 155.
— nutmeg peach, 121.
— Quarenden apple, 91.

INDEX

Red spider, 49.
Reine Hortense cherry, 141.
Reinette Anana, 97.
— de Canada, 98.
Ribston Pippin, 101.
Right to remove trees, 2.
Rivers's list of apples for dwarf culture, 103.
Rivers's nut trees, 168.
Roman nectarine, 125.
Root grafting, 20.
— pruning, 35.
Royal Apricot, 110.
— Duke cherry, 141.
— George peach, 118.

Saddle grafting, 19.
St. Catherine's plum, 134.
Salway peach, 121.
Sawing, 28.
Saw fly, 50.
Scaring birds, 41.
Scarlet Acari, 49.
— Crofton, 94.
— Pearmain, 96.
Seedlings, 13.
Seedling pear, 61.
Seckle pear, 69.
Seed, melon, 182.
Shoulder grafting, 20.
Side grafting, 20.
Situation for an orchard, 2.
Slugs and snails, 52.
Small Black cherry, 143.
Smith's Newington peach, 119.
Soil for apricots, 107.
—, orchard, 3.
—, peaches, 111.
Splice grafting, 18.
Spring Grove codlin, 92.
Spurs, 27, 62, 63.
Stations, 9.
Standard trees, 31, 62.
Stag beetle, 45.

Stocks, 10 to 12, 16, 87, 126.
Storing almonds, 105.
— apples, 58.
— fruit, 56.
— pears, 58.
— pears in a greenhouse, 58.
— quinces and medlars, 58.
— nuts, 59, 170.
— medlars, 168.
Strawberries, 160.
Strawberry bank, 162.
— propagation, 161.
— seedling, 161.
— soil for, 160.
— varieties, 163-165.
Striking without severance, 15.
Sulphur, 44.
Summer Bergamot pear, 66.
— Golden Pippin, 91.
— Pearmain, 96.
— pruning, 26, 108, 114, 127.
Swan's egg pears, 67.

Table trellises, 31, 35.
Tartarian black cherry, 139.
Temperature for fruit-room, 56.
Thinning fruit, 63.
— apples, 89.
— apricots, 108.
— peaches, 115.
Thrips, 48.
Tiffany, 40.
Time for planting, 8.
Tinea, 51.
Toads and frogs, 54.
Tools, 55.
Tortrix, 54.
Training, 30.
— apple trees, 89.
— cherries, 137.
Trees dying, 45.
Trésor baking pear, 84.

Tying grafts, 17.

Utility of cherries, 138.

Variegated Crassane pear, 74.
Ventilation of fruit-room, 57.
Vertical cordon training, 35.
Very late pears, 77.
Vine scale, 47.
Vines, 176.
Violet Diaper plum, 132.
Violette Hâtive nectarine, 123.
— peach, 118.
— plum, 128.

Walberton Admirable peach, 121.
Walls, 4, 5.
Walnuts, 171.
Washington plum, 131.
Washes for trees, 44, 45, 49.
Wasps, 42.
Wedge grafting, 19.
Weevils, 53.
Wellington apple, 90.
Werder's early cherry, 139.
Whip grafting, 18.
White Astrakan apple, 91.
— Bullace plum, 135.
— heart cherry, 143.
— currants, 154.
William's Bon Chrétien, 66.
Windsor pear, 66.
Winesour, 133.
Winter Nelis pear, 74.
— pears, 72.
— pruning, 26, 108, 114, 127, 147.
Wood destroyers, 45, 46.

Zéphirine Grégoire pear, 73.

Frederick Warne & Co., Publishers.

BY ALEXANDER C. EWALD, ESQ.
Of Her Majesty's Record Office, and Editor of "The Civil Service Guide."

NEW HISTORICAL WORK FOR STUDENTS.
In large crown 8vo, price 6s., cloth, 650 pp.

The LAST CENTURY *of* UNIVERSAL HISTORY.
A Reference Book, containing an Annotated Table of Chronology, List of Contemporary Sovereigns, a Dictionary of Battles and Sieges, and Biographical Notes of Eminent Individuals, from 1767 to 1867.

In crown 8vo, price 4s. 6d. cloth gilt.

OUR CONSTITUTION: A Record of the Origin and Gradual Progress of the Laws and Government of the British Empire, with Short Explanations of all Legal Terms.

In crown 8vo, price 3s. 6d. each, cloth gilt.

A REFERENCE BOOK of ENGLISH HISTORY.
Containing Tables of Chronology and Genealogy, a Dictionary of Battles, lines of Biography, and a digest of the English Constitution, from the Invasion of Julius Cæsar to 1866.

In crown 8vo, price 2s. 6d., cloth. Revised by A. C. EWALD.

HOW WE ARE GOVERNED; or, The Crown, the Senate, and the Bench. By FONBLANQUE and HOLDSWORTH.

Fcap. 8vo, cloth limp, price 1s.

THE CIVIL SERVICE TEXT-BOOK of PRECIS.

In 48mo, price 1s., cloth gilt; or roan, pocket book style, with elastic band, 2s.

THE BIJOU GAZETTEER OF THE WORLD
Briefly describing, as regards Position, Area, and Population, every Country and State, their Sub-divisions, Provinces, Counties, principal Towns, Villages, Mountains, Rivers, Lakes, Capes, &c. By W. H. ROSSER. 30,000 References.

In crown 8vo, price 2s. 6d., cloth gilt.

CARPENTRY AND JOINERY: a Useful Manual for the Many. With Original and Practical Illustrations. By S. T. AVELING.

In oblong 8vo, price 2s., roan.

HOPPUS'S MEASURER. Enlarged and Revised; the Contents being given in Feet, Inches, and twelfth-parts of an Inch. Edited by WM. RICHARDSON.

Bedford Street, Covent Garden.

www.ingramcontent.com/pod-product-compliance
Lightning Source LLC
Chambersburg PA
CBHW021734220426
43662CB00008B/845